Rekindling the Hope of the Manger

An Advent Study

Evan Drake Howard

Judson Press © Valley Forge

for Carol

REKINDLING THE HOPE OF THE MANGER
Copyright © 1992
Judson Press, Valley Forge, PA 19482-0851

Unless otherwise indicated, the Scripture quotations contained herein are from the New Revised Standard Version of the Bible, copyrighted 1989 by the Division of Christian Education of the National Council of the Churches of Christ in the United States of America, and are used by permission. All rights reserved.

Other quotations are from:

Revised Standard Version of the Bible, copyrighted 1946, 1952, © 1971, 1973 by the Division of Christian Education of the National Council of the Churches of Christ in the U.S.A., and used by permission.

Library of Congress Cataloging-in-Publication Data

Howard, Evan Drake, 1955-
    Rekindling the hope of the manger / by Evan Drake Howard.
        p.   cm.
    Includes bibliographical references.
    ISBN 0-8170-1180-3
    1. Advent—Meditations. 2. Christmas—Meditations. I. Title.
BV40.H69   1991
242'.33—dc20   91-25326
                                                             CIP

The name JUDSON PRESS is registered as a trademark in the U.S. Patent Office.
Printed in the U.S.A.

Contents

Introduction

The next time you scan the entertainment section of the newspaper, notice how prominently the theme of romance is featured. Someone has said that *all* American movies are love stories.

That may be an exaggeration, but few would deny the power of romance not only in the films, but also in the art, music, and literature of the past and present. From the Shakespearean classics to *Wuthering Heights* to *La Bohème* to *Camelot,* romance has stimulated the creativity of authors and moved the hearts of audiences.

Everyone loves a love story. But why is this so? Why do we return again and again to such an overworked theme? What accounts for our insatiable interest in the triumphs and tragedies that accompany falling in love?

This book does not attempt to answer these questions but to address the deeper curiosity from which the questions arise. As a resource for personal spiritual growth and group study, the book explores the idea that the mystery of romance is rooted in the mystery of God.

This book is meant to shed light on the focal point of God's love story—the birth of Jesus Christ. The drama of Christmas broke into history nearly twenty centuries ago when Mary gave birth to her firstborn son and wrapped him in swaddling cloths and laid him in a manger in Bethlehem. God gives us this greatest of all love stories as a gift. The story inspires the best and the highest in human romance, and in life itself.

But the wonder of Christmas is that it still breaks into our lives today. When this happens, when we hear the story as if for the first time, the hope of the manger is rekindled within us.

This book was written to help people awaken to the genius of God's masterpiece of love. Such an awakening rekindles the kind of hope that our world desperately needs. It is hope grounded in faith, hope that enables people to persevere—even to flourish—amidst the ominous crises of these times. When received in a spirit of worship and expectation, this hope has the power to heal and renew, to liberate and transform.

Each chapter approaches Christ's birth from a different perspective, seeking to encourage a creative encounter with the birth's revelation of God. It is hoped that this encounter will enable people to respond to the Christmas story in the beauty and power of its profound simplicity. In such a response lies the possibility of new insight and growth, new depth and wholeness.

The book is designed for adult study groups, but is equally suitable for individual use. Along with chapters based on the classic lectionary texts for the season from Advent to Epiphany, I have included accompanying prayers and questions for reflection. The study can be adapted according to the calendar for a particular year.

The questions are intended to help individuals and groups ponder the Christmas mystery through thought and discussion. The goal of this process is to unify the response of mind and heart, to help people integrate biblical knowledge with life experience, thus leading those who seek spiritual renewal to find it during one of the church's richest seasons.

The book is meant to be a resource for ministry—a guide for discussion at church, a companion for the journey to Bethlehem at home, a gift under the tree for a friend or family member. During this holiday season, when people are more open to the gospel than at other times, it may also have potential for use in outreach.

As the hope of the manger is rekindled within us, may we discover with the apostle Paul that "it is the God who said, 'Let light shine out of darkness,' who has shone in our hearts to give the light of the knowledge of the glory of God in the face of Jesus Christ" (2 Corinthians 4:6).

one

Romancing the Hope of Christ

The wilderness and the dry land shall be glad,
    the desert shall rejoice and blossom;
like the crocus it shall blossom abundantly,
    and rejoice with joy and singing.
The glory of Lebanon shall be given to it,
    the majesty of Carmel and Sharon.
They shall see the glory of the LORD,
    the majesty of our God.

Strengthen the weak hands,
    and make firm the feeble knees.
Say to those who are of a fearful heart,
    "Be strong, do not fear!
Here is your God.
    He will come with vengeance,
with terrible recompense.
    He will come and save you."

Then the eyes of the blind shall be opened,
    and the ears of the deaf unstopped;
then the lame shall leap like a deer,
    and the tongue of the speechless sing for joy.
For waters shall break forth in the wilderness,
    and streams in the desert;

the burning sand shall become a pool,
and the thirsty ground springs of water;
the haunt of jackals shall become a swamp,
the grass shall become reeds and rushes.

A highway shall be there,
and it shall be called the Holy Way;
the unclean shall not travel on it,
but it shall be for God's people;
no traveler, not even fools, shall go astray.
No lion shall be there,
nor shall any ravenous beast come up on it;
they shall not be found there,
but the redeemed shall walk there.
And the ransomed of the Lord *shall return,*
and come to Zion with singing;
everlasting joy shall be upon their heads;
they shall obtain joy and gladness,
and sorrow and sighing shall flee away.

—Isaiah 35:1-10

Advent is a time for romance. As the new church year dawns and begins the movement toward Christmas, it inspires a longing for the divine that can only be described in the most intimate relational language. This is especially so when people grasp the full significance of the season.

Advent is a time of heightened emotion and enhanced possibility. Suddenly the limitations placed on the natural world dissolve and miracles happen. Angels announce good news. Light challenges the reign of darkness. A virgin gives birth to a son. There is a fantasy and a mystery to it all that is new every year. Advent captures the imagination and warms the heart.

But this is only a beginning. Advent sends a rush of images through expectant minds—excited children, gifts under the tree, wreaths in church, snow on the ground, the sound of familiar carols. When people focus on the finest qualities of this season, they cannot help but look forward to its coming and find joy in its arrival. For a four-week period of time, an aura of romance is created by the bells and the candles, the holly and the mistletoe. Hearts grow tender, reminding people of the lifetime quest to find romance if they do not have it, or to keep it if they do.

A Liaison with Hope

Romance, by its very nature, requires a sharing between persons. The treasures of the human spirit lie dormant unless shared with another. We long to know and be known in the context of a growing relationship. It is said that romance is "the spice of life," but even more so it is the spice of faith. Advent helps us remember this. It prepares us to hear again the greatest love story ever told. It calls us to respond with renewed openness to God's gift of Christ. It gives us the chance to see the world and ourselves in a whole new way. It invites us, at least for a moment, to leave all doubt and despair behind, that we might be transformed by hope.

Isaiah wrote the thirty-fifth chapter of his prophecy in order to initiate this transformation. He wanted to give people a vision of a new and better day. He wanted to help those with fearful hearts to find courage and those with feeble knees to find strength. Thus Isaiah wrote about a coming age in which the eyes of the blind would be opened. The deaf would hear. The lame would walk. The dumb would speak. Streams of water would burst forth in the desert. And God's people would know everlasting joy.

When Christ came as the promised Messiah, he fulfilled Isaiah's hope. But if this hope is to belong to modern people in the modern world, it must be courted anew. Advent offers a place to begin. It is the season for romancing the hope of Christ.

It Begins with Attraction

Some people may be more skilled than others in the art of developing a love relationship with another, but no matter how experienced or inexperienced we are as lovers, we all know that certain elements must be present in any romance.

One needed element is attraction. Two people must share a mutual interest—the desire to take the risk of relationship. The problems of a certain couple illustrate the point: The man asked his young lady, "If I proposed, would you say yes?" And she responded with similar caution, "If you knew I would say yes, would you propose?" If a romance is ever going to get off the ground, two people must act on their feelings for each other. The same truth applies to our relationship with the hope of the Advent season: We must be willing to risk actively responding to the attractiveness of Christ.

Isaiah's idea that God is in the process of creating a new world of peace and beauty in which all of God's people shall live is attractive in and of itself. But amidst the crisis and pain of the present world, we often fear that conditions are deteriorating rather than improving. In light of this problem, it must be remembered that Advent's hope never forces itself on anyone. The level of its attractiveness depends on the quality of a person's attention to God. To be a Christian is to know times when hope is felt so strongly that it can barely be contained. Hope undergirds the words and thoughts of prayer, no matter how tentatively or confidently offered. Hope speaks through a friend's comforting presence in a vulnerable moment. It takes root in the heart as the tongue once again sings the carols of Christmas.

Remember also that the attractiveness of Advent's

hope is subtle—as subtle as the new life growing in Mary's womb. Christ comes to make all things new, but he always lets people choose whether they want him to or not. The hope he brings is always available, but sometimes we must wait out the barrenness and persevere through the darkness of life before we find it.

Is Christ attractive? Yes he is—if we will let him be. He is as attractive as perfect love itself. But one can only discover this truth by joining, in reverence and awe, with all those who gather at Bethlehem's manger to welcome his birth. Advent helps us do this. It stirs the embers of our faith by reminding us of our roots in Christ, the one who entered the world long ago, but who continues to enter every heart that welcomes him today.

What Every Good Love Triangle Needs

Another element critical to the romance of the season is passion. An insightful psychologist once said that an effective love relationship is like a well-balanced triangle with each side representing an indispensable ingredient. On the bottom of the triangle is communication; on the left side is intimacy; on the right side is passion. If we do not find ways to keep the flame of desire lit, it will die altogether. The artist Jules Feiffer drew a series of sketches of a bored and unhappy couple sitting opposite each other. Neither of them stirs until the man asks his wife, "Do you believe in life after death?" She replies, "What do you call this?"[1]

Some time ago, *Idaho Magazine* carried a story about a man who took a fishing trip to Lake Crescent, leaving his wife, who was nine months pregnant, at home. He caught a big trout, bigger than any of his previous catches. He was elated! In his joy, he telegraphed his wife. The message read, "I've got one; weighs 7 pounds and is a beauty." The wife responded with a telegram of her own: "So have I; weighs 8 pounds, 4 ounces. Not a beauty—looks like you. Come home."

When the passion is gone, you no longer have romance; you have drudgery; you have boredom and stagnation. Instinctively, we all know how it happens, but often we feel powerless to stop it. It happens through neglect, through disinterest, through little things like unthinking criticisms and big things like unrealistic expectations.

The problem also emerges in the life of faith. Sadly, some people begin the Christian life with great enthusiasm, but then lose the vitality of their hope before it fully develops. Initially they find joy in worship and study, prayer and service, but as time goes on, other demands undermine their spiritual discipline. Work, recreation, or a multitude of competing interests become more important than faith, and soon the passion is gone.

Beyond this, faith can be painful; it sometimes raises more questions than it answers. Faith does not promise us a tension-free life. Nor does it protect us from tragedy or shield us from loss. When we are hurting and God seems distant, our faith can lose its passion.

In these moments, doubting seems safer than believing. Doubt, after all, raises no expectations. It remains always detached, always uncommitted, a refuge of invulnerability in a world where believing hearts, like loving hearts, can get broken. There is no passion in doubt.

Passion comes from the kind of faith that risks surrendering to the mystery of God. Reinhold Niebuhr called this faith the "impossible possibility." That was his way of speaking of faith as the ultimate paradox, the quality least likely to be found in a broken world, where nothing is certain and everyone's final destination is the grave. So understood, faith incorporates both recklessness and caution, both abandon and restraint.

To believe in a good God when life is often so bad requires a willingness to live with contradiction. Clear-cut answers elude us in the real world; ambiguity clouds our understanding. We can't explain why people must suffer at the hands of ruthless dictators and incurable diseases. We feel numb and perplexed when we see images on the evening news of drugs and guns, gangs and refugees, recessions and wars. Our anxiety increases when our job, our health, or someone we love is suddenly taken from us.

In a world so filled with tragedy, despair often overshadows hope, making faith impossible, since tragedy leads us to be skeptical about God and cynical about life.

The genius of Christianity is its unflinching realism in addressing the problems of our tragic human condition. Christianity offers no panaceas, no easy answers, to make the hurt go away; panaceas and easy answers only intensify the hurt.

Instead, Christianity meets paradox with paradox. Tragedy becomes triumph when almighty God enters the human condition and bonds intimately with it. The bonding occurs as the Almighty becomes Bethlehem's vulnerable Babe, Calvary's Man of Sorrows, and heaven's risen and victorious Savior.

God counters the paradox of human suffering with the paradox of suffering love. Rather than acting alone and using cosmic power to overcome evil, God enlists us in the fight. In the Christmas event, our Creator reaches out to form a partnership with us, that together we can learn courage and grow in character as we move toward the wholeness of redemption's completed story.

The story is full of paradox. Jesus comes to show us the power of weakness, the abundance of sacrifice, the profundity of simplicity, the security of surrender. He turns our thinking about God and life upside down. He tells us that the last will become first and that the greatest in his kingdom will be servants of all.

His gospel confounds our expectations; it is full of surprise and scandal. But that's why it is also full of hope and possibility, for the gospel announces that in losing our lives for Christ we find them, and in dying in him, and with him, we are born anew to eternal life.

Advent celebrates the paradox of the gospel. Reminding us that we can know God's love even in such a broken world, Advent points us to Jesus, who embodies and vindicates that love. Jesus' birth declares that to let impossibility have the last word solves nothing.

Submitting to cynicism and despair in the face of unanswerable questions and perplexing dilemmas only creates restlessness of heart. Impossibility cannot nurture the romance of hope; only a vital personal faith can do that, and God's love expressed in the manger has given faith's possibility the last word, now and forever.

Like a phoenix rising out of the ashes of uncertainty, faith creates a new future. It says yes to God, believing that with God's help something good can emerge even from brokenness and uncertainty. Advent proclaims that this vital faith can be found again, that faith's passion can be restored, no matter how much of it has been lost to life's haste and hurt. As Isaiah prophesied (35:6b-7):

> Waters shall break forth in the
>   wilderness,
> and streams in the desert;
> the burning sand shall become a pool,
>   and the thirsty ground springs of
>   water.

Simply stated, passionate faith gives rise to hope, and hope has the power to enliven our spirits, even amidst life's many moments of distress. But this only happens when we believe it can. Such belief begins with a renewed commitment to cultivate one's inner life through worship, prayer, and study, and it matures with further dependence on the Holy Spirit.

Advent declares that spiritual passion can return

or be born where now absent and can deepen where already present. The hope of the Messianic age, which Isaiah heralded, is not meant for some other people in some other place in some distant future. It is meant for us—for you and for me—here and now, amidst all of the promise and all of the pain of our ordinary yet sacred lives. This is the romance into which God calls us, a romance sustained by a third element—devotion.

The Difference Devotion Makes

Anyone who has ever tried to love another person over a long period of time knows how hard it can sometimes be. Several years ago, a book entitled *Intimate Partners* dealt with this problem in the context of marriage. The author, Maggie Scarf, made the point that often in intimate relationships the very qualities that first attracted one person to another become sources of conflict later on. The man who was initially attracted by the warmth and easy sociability of his spouse may, at some future point, redefine these same attributes as "loudness, intrusiveness, or shallowness"[2] in relating to others. The woman who at first valued her husband for his reliability and the sense of security he offered her may, farther down the line, reinterpret these same qualities as dull, boring, or constricting.

Many pitfalls such as these threaten to stifle romance. Only those sincerely devoted to keeping their love alive will be successful. Times of special attention and creativity are needed. During these times, the lovers can enjoy new adventures together, become vulnerable to each other in open conversation, explore troublesome issues, and share the memories and hopes that first gave birth to their relationship.

So it is with Christian faith. A season such as Advent calls us to remember why we believed in the first place and offers opportunity to restore the vitality of our devotion to Christ. This season does not suggest that relatedness to God will make all of our dreams come true. Nor does it offer glib panaceas for the struggles that come with being human. Rather, Advent stages a drama of hope before our eyes and invites us to participate. Advent does not emphasize what we must do, but what God has done. It does not instruct us on how to be joyful or loving; it describes an experience of love and joy and bids us to share in it. During Advent, God's redemptive intrusion into history is depicted in corporate worship through readings and hymns, burning candles and majestic anthems. And yet, the story of redemption falls on deaf ears if people are not devoted to hearing it in ever more personal, more integrative ways.

Several years ago, when Garrison Keillor's *A Prairie Home Companion* radio program was still on the air, he told a story about a couple named Florian and Myrtle Krebsbach. The Krebsbachs were so predictable that every Friday night of their married lives, Myrtle served the same meal—breaded fish fillets. But every Friday night, her husband would sit down at the table, take the first bite, savor it, and say, "Ah, Myrtle, that's the best you ever did." The Krebsbachs were married for forty-seven years, but every Friday night Florian would find something new to compliment about Myrtle's breaded fish fillets.[3] That comes to almost 2500 compliments! It was his way of showing his devotion and of keeping romance in the marriage.

In order for Christians to live in hope—in the kind of hope that makes a difference in and through us—we must find ways to maximize our experience of it. Hope can be disturbed by conflict with others. It can be weakened by a personal crisis or upset by the ridicule of a skeptical world.

But Advent comes to infuse Christian hope with new romance. It does this as we hear again the message that we worship a God who saves. Thus spoke Isaiah, and like him, we look forward to a day in which God will act decisively in history. The old order of darkness will be abolished; a new order of light will come. In this new era, there will be no more sorrow, and all of God's people will rejoice in the promise of their salvation.

Advent is the season for romancing this hope again, for storing it up in our spirits so that it will sustain us in all our moments of despair. The fulfillment of Isaiah's prophecy was revealed in the Christ who came— and who continues to come—to the world and to every believing heart. During this season we prepare with eager expectation to welcome him. Isaiah's prophetic message is true. All people shall see "the glory of the LORD, the majesty of our God."

Prayer for the First Sunday in Advent

Loving God, during these days of Advent, we meditate
upon the meaning of your coming.
We approach you in wonder and awe as we prepare to
welcome the Christ, whom you have so
sacrificially sent.

How thankful we are for his assurance that you do not
leave us alone—
Into our highest joys and satisfactions, you send light
and warmth.
Into our experiences of worship, you bring insight
and renewal.
Into our times of stress and uncertainty, you infuse
strength and faith.

We rejoice in your transforming work going on in us and
in the world, your work that nothing can stop.
We come to you as seekers, as curious children wanting
to explore the mysteries of your grace and love.
Like Mary and Joseph,
we seek to experience the Christmas miracle ourselves.
Like the shepherds,
we seek to worship at the manger in Bethlehem.
Like the angels,
we seek to join the multitude of the heavenly host to
sing glory to you in the highest.

Give us sensitive spirits, attentive minds, and receptive
hearts, we pray.
Begin your work in us anew, that we might reflect your
light and life in every environment in which we
find ourselves.
Show us how we may more fully receive the gift of Jesus,
who is the sign of your presence in the world.

Bring to our awareness the places in our inner spirits
where he has yet to enter—the places where we have
resisted him,
rejected him,
run from him.
Help us to invite him to enter now. Grant that during this
Advent season, we might hear his Word and
experience his grace as if for the first time, that
we might respond with renewed commitment.

O God, rekindle the romance of our faith.
Awaken us to the attraction and the passion and the
devotion of Jesus Christ.
Let his hope live in us, not for our own sake only, but
for the sake of your eternal kingdom both in heaven and
on earth.
In all things and in all ways, make us people who think
and act in peace, that the world may know of your
saving love. AMEN.

Questions for Reflection and Study

1. It could be said that romance is one of the Bible's major themes. Throughout REKINDLING THE HOPE OF THE MANGER the theme of romance is related to the meaning of Christ's coming. Can you cite other places in the Bible where the idea of romance is prominent? (See, for example, the book of Hosea and New Testament references to the church as the "Bride of Christ.")

2. The experience of Christian discipleship is often referred to as a journey or pilgrimage. How does the idea of faith as romance differ from or complement this?

3. There are times for most Christians when faith becomes ordinary, routine, perhaps even dull or boring. How and why does this happen? How might a new understanding of faith as romance help to remedy the problem? As you consider this question, discuss also how the Advent/Christmas/Epiphany seasons might enhance the romance of faith, and how this enhancement might be sustained throughout the year.

4. One of the criticisms raised by some observers of Christianity is that it can be overly individualistic. How might the theme of romancing the hope of Christ be applied to social problems and to the life of the world?

5. A perennial issue of debate is whether conditions on earth are getting better or worse. On the pessimistic side are the two following statements from well-known sources. Woody Allen has been quoted as saying, "More than any other time in history, mankind faces a crossroads. One path leads to despair and utter hopelessness. The other to total extinction. Let us pray

we have the wisdom to choose correctly." Another cynical view comes from *The Denial of Death* by Ernest Becker, who writes, "Creation is a nightmare spectacular taking place on a planet that has been soaked for hundreds of millions of years in the blood of all its creatures. The soberest conclusion that we could make about what has actually been taking place on the planet for about three billion years is that it is being turned into a vast pit of fertilizer."[4] Explore another view by comparing the above statements with the biblical vision of hope as living (1 Peter 1:3), comprehensive (Romans 8:35-39), and certain (Revelation 21:1-4).

6. This chapter emphasizes the themes of attraction, passion, and devotion in the spiritual life. The suggestion is made that the highest use of these emotions is found in faith. But how are these same emotions misdirected in today's society? What else competes with Christ for our attraction, passion, and devotion? Read Matthew 6:19-24 and Luke 14:25-27. In light of all that competes for our attention today, what can we do to help us heed these words?

7. Discuss the paradox of a passionate faith—Niebuhr's "impossible possibility." How can Christianity's paradoxes overcome tragedy and despair with hope?

---

[1]From Robert M. Herhold, *The Promise Beyond the Pain* (Nashville: Abingdon Press, 1979), p. 83.

[2]Maggie Scarf, *Intimate Partners* (New York: Ballantine Books, 1988), p. 27.

[3]Found in Harold Hazelip and Ken Durham, *Jesus Our Mentor and Our Model* (Grand Rapids: Baker Book House, 1987), pp. 94-95.

[4]Ernest Becker, *The Denial of Death* (New York: The Free Press, a division of Macmillan Publishing Co., 1973), p. 283.

two

An Encompassing Comfort

Comfort, O comfort my people,
   says your God.
Speak tenderly to Jerusalem,
   and cry to her
that she has served her term,
   that her penalty is paid,
that she has received from the LORD's hand
   double for all her sins.

A voice cries out:
"In the wilderness prepare the way of the LORD,
   make straight in the desert a highway for our
      God.
Every valley shall be lifted up,
   and every mountain and hill be made low;
the uneven ground shall become level,
   and the rough places a plain.
Then the glory of the LORD shall be revealed,
   and all people shall see it together,
   for the mouth of the LORD has spoken."

—Isaiah 40:1-5

from Expectation to Experience

C.S. Lewis is remembered as one of the twentieth century's foremost Christian writers. Many, however, also remember him for something else: After a half-century as a confirmed bachelor, Lewis finally married. The story of Lewis's life with his American wife, Joy Davidman, is the subject of *Shadowlands,* a recent Broadway play by William Nicholson that dramatizes the promise and pain of that brief yet memorable romance. It was a romance made all the more poignant by Joy's struggle against cancer, a struggle she ultimately lost.

One of the underlying themes of *Shadowlands* also emerges in the meaning of Advent. The theme suggests that when romance reaches its highest levels of maturity and intimacy, it can become a profound source of comfort in the face of suffering and pain. In this sense, the comfort of deep and abiding love, the love that is romance at its best, can become a sign of inner hope when all outer hope has died.

In the "shadowlands" of this mortal existence, believed Lewis, such comfort reveals God's presence. Thus, after Joy's death, Lewis would write, "It is incredible how much happiness, even how much gaiety, we sometimes had together after all hope was gone. How long, how tranquilly, how nourishingly, we talked together that last night!"[1]

The comfort that is at the heart of Lewis's words is also at the heart of Advent. As the fortieth chapter of Isaiah suggests, Advent holds forth the possibility that we can find an encompassing comfort even in the "shadowlands" of our lives. This possibility increases as hope becomes tangible, allowing human beings to catch the scent of its romance.

During Advent, expectation ends in experience. When the season climaxes in the Christmas event, the universal is revealed in the particular, the majestic in the mundane. The Advent hope of a coming comfort is marked by progression. It begins as a faint whisper of

Majesty in a Manger

promise amidst prophetic thunderings of judgment. It grows gradually into a vision, a daring dream of cosmic newness. Then, at just the right moment, in the fullness of time, when life's longing for fulfillment can no longer be contained, hope emerges from Mary's womb, visible, physical, alive and breathing, the Word made flesh.

Comfort is an active expression of the hope of Christ. It is the general made specific, the abstract made concrete. The concreteness of Emmanuel, God with us, restores the heart's capacity to feel, to bear the risks of fervent affection. Only in the security of this solid hope can the journey toward enriched faith continue.

When Grief Draws Near, Despair Draws Nigh

In the days just prior to Advent each year, Americans remember a national tragedy—the assassination of President John F. Kennedy. Most people who were living at the time can recall exactly where they were on November 22, 1963. As the nation watched the televised coverage of the state funeral, grief set in. The first family all in black, the riderless horse ahead of the flag-draped casket, the President's young son offering a final salute— these images weighed heavily upon the national spirit. It has been said that some of the best sermons ever preached in America were delivered from the country's pulpits on the Sunday following the assassination. We were grieving, and we needed help.

Such an outpouring of corporate emotion is rare; personal struggles with grief are not. Amidst the losses of our lives, we long for the kind of comfort that eases the pain, that stills the questions, that dispels the anger, that lifts the despair. Life brings moments in which people are staggered by the winds of disappointment or buffeted by the rising tide of defeat. In such moments, high hopes turn from being realizable possibilities that empower, to being haunting voices that mock. Unexpected betrayals and inexplicable tragedies, lingering hurts and perplexing crises, gnawing loneliness and shattered expectations—how dark is the path a person must sometimes walk.

When confronted with these painful realities, some contemporary thinkers advocate submission to despair. It is more realistic, they counsel, to curse the darkness than to light a candle. Ironically, Samuel Beckett, the Nobel Prize–winning writer whose work epitomized the modern romance with despair, died during Advent in 1989, only three days before Christmas, which celebrates hope. "There are no landmarks in my work," Beckett once said. "We must invent a world in which to survive, but even this invented world is pervaded by fear and guilt. Our existence is hopeless."[2]

Beckett's vision of life's barrenness culminated in his play *Waiting for Godot,* a two-act story about two tramps, Gogo and Didi, waiting for a third. The arrival of a cruel fat man driving a slave with a heavy burden catches them off guard. He is not Godot. The crisis he causes only temporarily interrupts their grim jokes and pitiful attempts to entertain themselves. The pathos of the tramps' questions about their despairing existence intensifies when Gogo, staggering, asks his friend, "Do you think God sees me?" Didi answers, "You must close your eyes." Gogo does, and staggers even more. If God exists at all, suggests Beckett in his play, then God is like Godot, an offstage presence who suspends humanity in the limbo of meaninglessness, and who never comes to bring comfort.

Isaiah's Vision— An Inviting Alternative

Beckett's message contrasts sharply with the hope that permeates the Advent season. Isaiah bears witness to God's comforting character and actions. Not only in times

He shows up!

of crisis, not only in experiences of corporate sorrow, but also in the everyday stresses and struggles of life, God's presence brings comfort. As a gift of grace, the divine presence enfolds people in love.

True, the world often seems like a comfortless place. Impersonal economic and social systems remain indifferent to human pain. Wars rage. The balance of power favors the "haves," while the "have-nots" fall through the cracks. In many places, people are undernourished and underemployed, undereducated and underclothed, undersheltered and underloved.

But Isaiah speaks of a reality that goes deeper than worldly problems. His words are not meant to soothe as much as to exhort and challenge. "Comfort, O comfort, my people" is analogous to Jesus' New Testament statement, "Take heart! I have overcome the world." It is an imperative, another way of saying, "Fear not! Stand firm! Be of good courage!"

Moses spoke similar words to the Israelites as they fled the Egyptians. Elijah spoke likewise to the widow at Zarephath as she and her young son faced possible starvation. Haggai, Nehemiah, and Zechariah also used imperatives in encouraging the returned exiles as they faltered before the task of rebuilding the temple.

"Comfort, O comfort, my people" is Isaiah's call for faith and character in the face of impending despair. As he develops his message further, he sets forth the foundation on which the possibility of comfort stands. A transforming revelation of God is coming. Old things will pass away; all will be made new. Warfare will end. Past sins will be forgiven. Fear will become courage; weakness will become strength.

> "Every valley shall be lifted up,
>   and every mountain and hill be made low;
> the uneven ground shall become level,
>   and the rough places a plain.

> Then the glory of the LORD shall be revealed,
> and all people shall see it together,
> for the mouth of the LORD has spoken."
>
> —Isaiah 40:4-5

Advent anticipates the revelation of glory that Isaiah foresaw. Christians believe that the prophet's transforming vision found its fulfillment in Bethlehem's manger. Nothing could stop God's glory from being revealed in Christ—not the sins of the world, not the hardened hearts of the people, not the callousness of history.

The glory of Christ makes hope personal. Hope is God's comforting presence in the infant Savior. Christ's incarnation makes obsolete all concepts of God as aloof or capricious, distant or dead. No longer is life the story of waiting for a divine coming that never takes place. In Christ, God has come and will come again.

The romance Christ offers includes no fluctuation of feeling, one day intense and passionate, the next reserved and tentative. The transcendent yet immanent lover continually woos his beloved. Christ invites all people to respond in turn, to nurture the romance, to demonstrate it in loving attitudes, to bear witness to it in acts of justice and peace.

Isaiah interprets this romantic impulse as all-encompassing comfort. This comfort is as real as the earth itself, as dependable as the arrival of night and day. It has a moral component that sensitizes the conscience; a theological component that stimulates the mind; a spiritual component that calms the soul; an existential component that affirms life in its wholeness.

Even though comfort is revealed with new immediacy and power in God's Messiah, it remains inaccessible unless claimed by perceptive people who welcome it into the real world of their daily experience. Few are given tangible evidence of the divine presence. Most human crises happen far from the sights and sounds of angels visitant or opening skies. Instead, comfort comes in the

God's got something for you.

form of faith, the assurance of things hoped for, the conviction of things not seen.

Toward a Fuller Revelation of Truth

Like all else in the spiritual life, God's comfort is already present yet still to come. Prophets predicted its possibility; Christ embodied its reality. But its fullness will not be made complete until time passes into eternity. Emphasizing this truth, the apostle Paul wrote, "For now we see in a mirror, dimly, but then we will see face to face. Now I know only in part; then I will know fully, even as I have been fully known" (1 Corinthians 13:12).

Human experience and knowledge are always partial, limited by the boundaries of mortality. Spiritual truth must be discovered in bits and pieces. It remains tantalizingly beyond the hand's grasp and the heart's embrace. Advent does not bemoan this fact, but celebrates it. Sharpening the focus of the Christian life, Advent declares that faith grows through participation, not passivity.

Advent bathes in realism the path toward God, refusing to offer glib ecstasy or easy discipleship as a way of attracting new adherents. It portrays the Christian experience exactly as it is—a discipline of waiting, searching, following; a pilgrimage toward a completeness achieved only through enduring the trials of incompleteness.

Nothing happens all at once. The movement toward spiritual maturity takes time. So it is with the Advent season. It progresses slowly through *chronos* time (minutes, hours, days) to *kairos* time (a moment of God's intervention). It presses deliberately and inexorably toward its objective. Those who benefit from it most are people attuned to its meaning. They live the season expectantly but also patiently, seizing the opportunity for quietness before the coming God, responsive to the Spirit's work in the world and in their lives.

The Advent hope becomes a dynamic force for

change when related to the meaning of Jesus Christ. Isaiah's proclamation of comfort culminated in the promised Messiah. The oft-quoted statement is true: Christ came to comfort the disturbed and to disturb the comfortable. The holy birth that took place in Bethlehem was meant both to console and to constrain, both to heal and to convict. The religious people of Jesus' day had become too comfortable in their self-righteousness. The wealthy had become too comfortable in their possessions. The powerful had become too comfortable in their authority. Jesus came to preach a provocative message and to carry out a revolutionary mission.

To paraphrase the opening theme of his Sermon on the Mount as recorded by Luke, "Woe to you who are on top and in control now, because the day is coming when the tables will be turned and a new order of justice and equality will be established." In this coming order, taught Jesus, a new ethic would govern the actions of God's people, an ethic of turning the other cheek, of showing love to enemies, of doing unto others as one would have others do likewise.

There is comfort in the knowledge that the future belongs to Jesus Christ. Isaiah 40 envisions the triumph of his values, the inevitability of his reign. He comes to reveal truth, the basis of all authentic security. Truth perseveres in the face of injustice. It endures in spite of international terrorism and sectarian violence. It stands against racist structures and attitudes. Truth outlasts domestic abuse and oppressive addictions and escapist materialism. It reigns over every evidence of personal or social evil. In Christ, truth is in the process of vindicating right and defeating wrong. Truth may be crushed in Tiananmen Square in Beijing, but it rises again in Wenceslas Square in Prague.[3] It may submit to a cruel death on Calvary only to win victory over the grave on Easter Sunday morning.

When life is aligned with truth, it has meaning,

and where there is meaning, there is comfort. As long as I know that beneath the confusion and pain of the world lies a deeper rational order; as long as I can find hope in sorrow as well as joy; as long as I can experience the sacred even in secular things—then I claim my inalienable personhood and live with purpose in all circumstances. Here emerges the comfort of spiritual knowledge, the knowledge that life originates and flourishes in a God who graciously shares the gift of fullness with all who seek it. During Advent, this gift is awaited with intensifying drama, reaching its denouement in the Savior's birth.

"Onement" as a Christian Possibility

Advent brings hope not because it promises to make life perfect, but because it aspires to make it holy— the very place of God's visitation. The miraculous birth that Advent foreshadows preserves life's potential for both redemption and transformation. Christ came in order to advance God's work of creating a new heaven and a new earth.

Jesus brings God's salvation. His presence in the world introduces an alternative to panic as a response to uncertainty. The very idea of a Savior, a Christ figure who comes to deliver the world from injustice and set people free, is deeply comforting. Stock prices may fluctuate on Wall Street; foreign governments may rise and fall; natural catastrophes may devastate large geographical areas, wreaking havoc on vulnerable populations. But as long as time continues, God's redemptive work will not be thwarted. Instead, that work will energize the process by which the unity and peace of Christ will finally come to all things.

Isaiah's Advent message of comfort is rooted in this assurance of ultimate salvation. Now even the hardest experiences of life are not beyond redemption. God enters into the human experience at the point of its extremity, at the point where all hope seems gone, all endurance spent. The reality of Christ's birth means that loneliness can give way to friendship, isolation to community, quiet despair to resurgent joy.

Advent reminds the world of God's nearness in Christ. Its promise of comfort defies description by word or concept; it ascends to the level of art. A modern painting by the American artist Barnett Newman expresses the mystery of discordant elements joining together to create a new, unified whole. Entitled *Onement,* this innovative work by Newman shows an "incompleted image, with one color crossed vertically by a strip of paint which both divides and joins its symmetrical left and right sides."[4] The painting was Newman's first after a long period of inactivity during which he had become disillusioned with the predictability of traditional European art. *Onement* represents an attempt at redefinition, a radical experiment in starting afresh, an opportunity to introduce new levels of imaginative meaning into the twentieth century's artistic awareness.

Advent is also a movement toward "onement," toward a perfect intersection of the human and the divine in Christ. All of the discordant elements that cause tension between the finite and the infinite, the mortal and the immortal, are harmonized into a state of creative integration in the miraculous birth at Bethlehem. The image of God, present but obscured in each person and in nature, finds its fulfillment in the Christ who blends the contrasting colors of divinity and humanity into a radiant and indissoluble "onement." By obedience to God's will, Jesus overcame—and in him, we overcome—the incongruities of matter and spirit, weakness and strength, purity and sin. Oneness—the union of the human with God—becomes real in the incomparable wonder of the incarnation.

The reason that Advent possesses such a spirit of hope and comfort has to do with the intimate fusion of the eternal and the temporal in the infant Jesus. This spirit of intimacy emanates from the truth that in Christ, God is with us now and forever—with us to encourage, to support, to heal. There is no greater comfort than the knowledge that we are not alone, that nothing "in all creation will be able to separate us from the love of God in Christ Jesus our Lord" (Romans 8:39).

Comfort, as an element of God's great romance with humanity, permeates the Advent season, animating the spiritual quest. Two truths infuse passion into the life of faith: An encounter with God is no longer a distant dream, and human beings can achieve new levels of inner awareness because of Christ's coming. Indeed, the stillness of a Judean night brought passionate fulfillment to one of humanity's fondest hopes—the hope that romance is near, that its mystery and wonder are meant for everyone, and that it is stronger than any deprivation, any oppression. Advent invites us into the kind of renewed faith that nurtures the flame of this romance; it offers opportunity for a new level of intimacy in our relationship with God. Here there is no fear of a broken heart. The human longing for communion with another discovers its highest purpose as God's beloved emerges from the Virgin's womb. Relatedness to him means security, completion, and peace. His presence initiates a celebration of cosmic newness. In the Christ, who is God's sign of love for the world, hope becomes comfort, and romance becomes real.

Prayer for the Second Sunday in Advent

O God of promise and fulfillment, your faithfulness is
    great.
No matter how far we stray from you, you refuse to forget
    us.
In your presence, we would
    take off our masks,
        put aside our pretensions,
            and lay bare our real selves.
We wait for you in faith, trusting that you will make
    yourself known in the still, small voice of your
    Spirit.

As we meditate upon the appearing of our Lord Jesus, we
    give thanks for the hope of comfort and the
    comfort of hope he brings.
We approach the manger of Bethlehem as pilgrims who
    stand in half-belief, profoundly stirred.

We look into the stable and see in the stillness him who
    comes to share our every struggle, our every
    concern.
We know, O Lord, that without him we would be lost,
    for we would have no truth to guide us,
        no grace to sustain us,
            no incarnate Word to heal and redeem us.

Prepare our hearts to receive your Christ, O God.
Renew our awareness of the comfort he brings, a comfort
    not of noble intentions only, but of promises
    made and kept.

As recipients of his love and grace, guard us from
    complacency.

May we be quick to share with others the comfort with
which we ourselves have been comforted, that
your peace may come to all people.
Purge from our hearts any dissatisfaction, known or
unknown, that inhibits us from being at peace with
you.
Free us from desiring to become ever more comfortable
while others suffer.
Instead, fill us with holy and passionate discomfort
in the presence of injustice,
in the sight of prejudices both blatant and subtle,
in the awareness of hatred as both potential evil
and present danger.
Empower us to stand against these wrongs, we pray.
Sustain us with the promise that the future belongs to
you, that one day all wars will cease, all conflicts
end, and the kingdoms of this world will become
the kingdom of our God and of his Christ.
Disturb us with this comfort, that we might serve your
kingdom more diligently and consistently than
we serve ourselves, our insatiable needs, our
unholy greeds.
As Advent progresses and we prepare to rejoice in Christ's
birth, help us to recognize him as the one in
whom your kingdom comes, that we might live
in hope and help others to hope as well. AMEN.

Questions for Reflection and Study

1. It has been said that while other religions emphasize humanity's search for God, Christianity stresses God's search for humanity. Do you agree with this statement? If not, why? If so, how is this borne out by the meaning of the Advent/Christmas/Epiphany season?

2. The idea of God comforting people is found in many significant biblical passages. Read the following texts and discuss the variety of ways comfort and hope are related.
   Psalm 23:4: Comfort as the hope of protection.
   Isaiah 51:3: Comfort as the hope of renewal.
   Isaiah 61:1-3 and Matthew 5:4: Comfort as the hope of deliverance from grief.
   2 Corinthians 1:3-7: Comfort as the hope of perseverance through crisis.

3. Do you understand God's comfort more as a feeling that people experience or as an attitude they develop as an outgrowth of faith? Can it be both? If so, what is the relationship between the two?

4. There are many times in life when people who are in need of God's comfort feel alienated from it. What might be the cause of this? How is the meaning of Advent relevant to the experience of waiting for comfort? In reflecting on these questions, supplement the message of Isaiah 40 with readings from Psalms 25:1-7; 27:7-14; and 40:1-5.

5. The need for comfort often comes from some kind of suffering, whether psychological, emotional, or physical; and suffering is often caused by the presence of

evil in the world. Reflect on the meaning of Advent for the problem of suffering, and do so in light of the following two statements. The first is by the South African author Alan Paton, who lived all his life with the suffering caused by apartheid. The second is from a sermon by William Sloane Coffin, a former minister at Riverside Church in New York City, shortly after the death of his son, Alex.

All who are mature, whether young or old, accept suffering as inseparable from life; even if it is not experienced, the possibility of it is always there. I myself cannot even conceive of life without suffering. I cannot even conceive that life could have meaning without suffering. There would certainly be no music, no theatre, no literature, no art. I suspect that the alternative to a universe in which there is suffering, in which evil struggles with good and cruelty with mercy, would be a universe of nothingness . . . only an eternity of uninterrupted banality.[5]

Nothing so infuriates me as the incapacity of seemingly intelligent people to get it through their heads that God doesn't go around in this world with his finger on triggers, his fist around knives, his hands on steering wheels. God is dead set against all unnatural deaths. And Christ spent an inordinate amount of time delivering people from paralysis, insanity, leprosy, and muteness. . . . The one thing that should never be said when someone dies is, "It is the will of God." Never do we know enough to say that. My own consolation lies in knowing that it was not the will of God that Alex die; that when the waves closed over the sinking car, God's heart was the first of all our hearts to break.[6]

[1]C.S. Lewis, *A Grief Observed* (New York: Harper and Row Publishers, 1961), p. 25.

[2]Quoted in Charles Campbell, "Samuel Beckett, Playwright, Winner of Nobel Prize; at 83," *Boston Globe,* December 27, 1989, p. 67.

[3]I am indebted to "The Independence Decade," *Wall Street Journal,* December 28, 1989, p. 48, for this thought.

[4]See Christopher Andreae, "Modern Art 'From Scratch,' " *Christian Science Monitor,* November 2, 1989, pp. 16-17.

[5]Alan Paton, "Why Suffering?" In *Creative Suffering: The Ripple of Hope* (Kansas City: National Catholic Reporter Publishing Co., 1970), p. 15.

[6]William Sloane Coffin, "Alex's Death," a sermon preached at Riverside Church on January 23, 1983. From Kent D. Richmond, *Preaching to Sufferers: God and the Problem of Pain* (Nashville: Abingdon Press, 1988), p. 69.

three

A Death Knell for Defeat

Sing aloud, O daughter Zion;
  shout, O Israel!
Rejoice and exult with all your heart,
  O daughter Jerusalem!
The LORD has taken away the judgments against
      you,
  he has turned away your enemies.
The king of Israel, the LORD, is in your midst;
  you shall fear disaster no more.
On that day it shall be said to Jerusalem:
Do not fear, O Zion;
  do not let your hands grow weak.
The LORD, your God, is in your midst,
  a warrior who gives victory;
he will rejoice over you with gladness,
  he will renew you in his love;
he will exult over you with loud singing
  as on a day of festival.

—*Zephaniah 3:14-17*

"Dear Rabbi, I want to thank you for the beautiful way you brought my happiness to a conclusion." A disgruntled bridegroom's thank-you note to the rabbi who had officiated at his wedding indicates how easily love goes sour. Once conflict sets in, romantic attachments can become hostile embattlements. It happens often. In this case, the wife's attitude caused the problem. She said to her husband, "All right, I will admit I was wrong if you will admit I was right."

Those are fighting words. They are descriptive of the potential for conflict that lurks in the shadows of every romance. It takes a certain amount of courage (some might say foolhardiness) to allow one's heart to become attached to another's. Such attachments involve vulnerability, and only the courageous can sustain them.

Beyond Conflict to Deepened Relationship

When love is new and innocent, it is easy to trust it, submitting to its seductions and embracing its charms. But sooner or later there comes a time when the ease ends and turns to trouble instead. Even the best relationships have their share of conflict. The joys of affection cannot be won without the cost of pain.

Advent tells the world that it also takes courage to believe, that discovering the romance of the manger requires abandoning fear. Even more, Advent identifies the source of courage and invites all people to draw near to it, that they might renew their strength.

Finding the source of our courage, our means of dispelling fear, leads us to a greater sense of security. The prophet Zephaniah propels the season's movement toward Christmas by emphasizing the security that God provides for those who live by faith. This security is rooted in the courtship that God initiated with humanity in creation and has continued through time. The Bible contains the record of the courtship, the details of both exalted communion and combative discord.

The end of Zephaniah's third chapter strikes a recurring Advent theme: God's love is a renewing presence. When people receive it, they find the courage that is a gift of hope. But renewal cannot come to any romance unless the lovers honestly confront their issues of conflict. Such confrontation either draws the couple closer together or pulls them apart. Whatever happens, when relational conflicts are faced, they unleash volatile emotions. The destiny of the people involved may hang in the balance.

This theme of love being renewed through the resolution of conflict is so timeless that it has inspired countless dramas on stage and screen. One recent play, A.R. Gurney's *Love Letters*, uses a unique form to demonstrate the theme's power. The play requires no acting, memorized lines, or elaborate staging. It relies only on the willingness of a man and a woman to share their lives with each other through letters written over a fifty-year period.

The two characters, an idealistic Republican senator and an accomplished but spoiled, alcoholic artist, sit at a desk and read to each other from their years of correspondence. As they share their personal pilgrimages through school and work, broken marriages, and nervous breakdowns, they interact at various times as friends, siblings, or lovers. The actors never leave the desk or even look at each other, but their attempts to express their feelings and resolve their conflicts through the letter readings touch the heights and depths of human emotion.

In suggesting that the richness of love between two people far exceeds the satisfactions of success in art or politics, *Love Letters* affirms the possibility and pain of intimacy. The reason for the play's popularity may well stem from its roots in the divine drama of God's love for all, from which romance between the sexes draws its inspiration.

It was this theme of the triumph of the divine romance that inspired Zephaniah as he envisioned the future of Israel. A conflict had developed between God and the people because they had fallen into idolatry. Forsaking their covenant commitments, they had played the harlot with foreign deities and tolerated festering injustice in their land. As the last prophet to urge repentance before the coming judgment at the hands of the Babylonians, Zephaniah warned of the terrible day of God's wrath. But before he finished, he tempered his message with words of hope about a coming age in which his people would find courage in God's triumphant love.

When God's Hiddenness Causes Conflict

Zephaniah was more than a prophet; he was a pastor with a counselor's insight. With keen diagnostic skill he observed that the life of faith can lose its romance as easily as can the life of love. Faith grew cold among his people not so much because of neglect, but because of fear. The Israelites who lived in Judah in the seventh century B.C. had seen their nation decline economically and militarily while neighboring countries were gaining strength. It was natural for them to be afraid. They trembled at the thought of failed crops, political instability, and future defeat at the hands of foreigners.

They also feared that walking the straight and narrow in covenant with Yahweh would leave them feeling bored and stifled rather than satisfied and whole. Other gods seemed to offer more security, not to mention more fun. So Zephaniah's people threw caution to the wind and sowed the wild but forbidden oats of infidelity. Yielding to unfaithfulness, they demonstrated the truth that the opposite of love is not hate, but fear.

Our problem is much the same. We cannot see or

touch God, or even prove God exists. Amidst such existential uncertainty, life can be frightening. Accidents happen; relationships falter; injustices strike; sorrows intrude. To paraphrase psychiatrist M. Scott Peck, "The only security that can be depended upon is life's insecurity."

In violent times like ours, the problem of God's hiddenness is especially acute because it raises questions about the practicality of faith. When a murder is committed every twenty-four minutes, a burglary every ten seconds, and a rape every seven minutes, as is the case in America today, people are justifiably afraid. They ask the same question raised by the Israelites of Zephaniah's day, "Where is God?" Moreover, in the face of problems such as hunger and homelessness, apartheid and terrorism, drugs and AIDS, economic upheavals and environmental crises, they wonder if it makes sense to believe in the ultimate triumph of goodness at all.

Many can relate to an incident from the life of Theresa of Avila, a sixteenth-century nun in the Carmelite order. One day she and fifty of her fellow sisters were traveling on foot to a neighboring convent during a terrible storm. When they came to a dangerously unstable bridge that provided the only way across a swollen stream, they paused to pray, led by St. Theresa. She asked that the bridge might hold up until they were safely across, but it didn't. Just as the nuns got to the middle, it collapsed, spilling them all into the water below. After they had struggled to shore, Theresa raised her eyes to heaven and said, "Lord, if this is the way you treat your friends, it is little wonder you have so many enemies!"

The people of Zephaniah's day also faced disheartening circumstances. At one time they had lived in communion with God, faithful in worship and attentive in service. They had been nurtured in the Law and its traditions; they knew they were loved. They had seen God's power at work in their leaders; they knew they were people of the promises. But over time they had begun to interpret God's hiddenness as God's absence. Gone were the cloud by day and the pillar of fire by night. Amidst feelings of abandonment and neglect, their faith lost its romance, and the temptation to pursue illicit liaisons with idols became too strong to resist.

At one level their unfaithfulness is easy to understand. They wanted faith's romance on their own terms, not God's. Consequently, when their desires for an easier, more exciting life went unfulfilled, they chose to seek fulfillment elsewhere.

The Season That Brings God Near

Advent can prevent us from making the same mistake that Zephaniah's people made. Advent's message is one of visitation, not abandonment. When immersed in the struggles of life, we need desperately to hear God say, "I love you." Our very well-being depends upon the sincerity and dependability of those words. The good news is that the "I love you" of God resonates in every aspect of Advent, from its spirit of expectation to its aura of mystery. And this message of affection is not heard faintly or distantly, but clearly and unmistakably in the power of the Christmas story.

Advent is a yearly reminder of God's nearness. It comes as predictably as December's brisk winds and cold temperatures. It arrives just when we need it most, just when nature's severity, like the severity of life's pressures, threatens to overwhelm us. In the winter of our vulnerability, when days are short and spirits low, when the thickening darkness casts shadows on life's goodness and hope, Advent announces that God has not forgotten us, that even in our most desolate moments, we are upheld by the everlasting arms. Advent is the season in which God's love returns to renew the weary and strengthen the weak. All who respond find their commitment deepened, their worship enriched.

Putting the matter vividly, Zephaniah presents the details of Advent's promise. The promise brings rejoicing. After a time of estrangement, the sacred union between God and God's beloved people is consummated again. The romance that had died is now rekindled; singing and gladness replace depression and grief.

Zephaniah suggests that God has sounded the death knell for defeat. In the coming messianic age, God's people shall live in the courage that is a gift of hope. This new courageous spirit, however, will not arise from their own efforts, but from God's initiative. In the promised Savior, the Lord himself is in our midst, a warrior who gives victory.

Many sensitive Christians are uncomfortable with Old Testament images of warfare and battle. As followers of the Prince of Peace, they should be. But the idea of God being on the side of his people, reaching out to help them when they need it most, is not offensive, but empowering. This is Zephaniah's deeper message. He heralds the Messiah's advent by announcing a future age in which the faithful win victory in their triumphant Lord.

Advent teaches that the fullness of God's revelation is to be found in what's ahead of us, not what's behind us. Jesus' birth in Bethlehem is to be celebrated not as a final declaration of God's defeat of evil, but as part of the process by which the victory will finally be won. Advent points us to the future even more than to the past. It declares that even as history is the place of revelation, so will eternity be the place of fulfillment.

How ironic that a helpless infant in a manger promises so much security—the security of knowing that the future will bring the triumph of goodness and peace, and that God will embrace us in it. Neither the best of our own efforts nor the might of the most sophisticated weapons can make a similar promise. This is the joyous contradiction that we celebrate every year during Advent. The dawning of the Christian year says that the future is

God's and that Christ comes to bring it to us in the present. No wonder Zephaniah could say:

> Sing aloud, O daughter Zion;
> shout, O Israel!
> Rejoice and exult with all your heart,
> O daughter Jerusalem!

Victory over Judgment

There are three areas in which Zephaniah's message sounds defeat's death knell. It is first announced that God takes the side of believers when they face judgment. Amidst the reproofs and condemnations of life, people of faith have a place to turn. They need not cower under even the severest scrutiny, whether it comes from God or others or themselves.

True, there are occasions on which our actions deserve strong critique and correction, but at other times we are judged unfairly. One of the reasons that many people lack self-confidence is that they never feel they quite meet someone else's standards—even when they are giving their best.

There is a story about a pianist who was an admirer of the renowned composer George Gershwin. When Gershwin died, this pianist decided to write a musical tribute in his honor. Having completed the arrangement, he took it to one of Gershwin's closest friends, Oscar Levant, and played it for him. After the young pianist had finished, he looked to Levant for approval. Levant's response was, "I think it would have been better if you had died and Gershwin had written the tribute!"

Such judgments fall hard upon sensitive human ears. Whether deserved or not, they say, "You don't measure up! Your gifts and efforts are second-rate at best!" No one completely escapes this kind of derision. There are moments when who we are or what we have done comes under judgment. We don't always fit in with the crowd; we suffer the chastisement of rejection. Others ridicule our choices or decisions. Sometimes we neglect responsibilities or fail in relationships, turning friends into enemies. At other times we agonize over secret sins or unconquered passions and suffer under the weight of self-accusation and guilt. This is where defeat begins. It takes root when a person believes the worst. A crack forms in the restraining wall of the psyche, and the integrity of the self comes under attack.

Zephaniah knew that to live under judgment is to be broken and joyless. Therefore he emphasized God's mercy. Heaven's displeasure will not last forever, nor will wrath be the final message from on high. A Savior comes to set all things aright, to break Adam's curse by bearing God's judgment himself. Born in a humble stable, he is the Lamb of God, who takes away the sin of the world. In calling attention to his appearing, Advent announces freedom, a new opportunity for people to walk in grace, forgiven in Christ, reconciled to God, living witnesses to the hope of peace on earth, good will to all.

Victory over Evil Enemies

The romance of the manger cannot be claimed apart from Zephaniah's second affirmation. A realist, he recognized that people of faith have enemies, that they face opposition from adversaries ever close at hand. Life is not always friendly. We are imperfect people in an imperfect world, and the existence of evil makes conflict inevitable. To name one's enemies takes a high degree of self-awareness; to face them takes courage.

Some enemies are distant and impersonal—a hostile foreign government, an inner-city crime ring, a social system that institutionalizes racism, sexism, and militarism. Other enemies lurk beneath life's surface, conveniently ignored until they strike with devastating force—enemies such as sickness and suffering and death.

People are also potential foes. The disagreeable co-worker, the disgruntled neighbor, the spiteful spouse or relative, the former friend with a penchant for rumor-mongering—how brutal are the wars these adversaries can wage. Even worse, internal spiritual enemies afflict us all. They are the temptations that besiege us, the hurts and regrets that plague us, the unfulfilled dreams that haunt us.

Zephaniah's message is clear. No enemy can stand against the God who renews people in love. Every ally of evil will eventually be overthrown and God will reign supreme. When people hear and believe this message of inevitable triumph, they find strength to fight their daily battles.

During Advent, this message becomes prominent. Even the powers of hell will not prevail against the eternal kingdom that Christ comes to establish. His love sounds the death knell for evil and its emissaries. Advent challenges Christians to respond to Christ's love, to incorporate it into their lives so fully that it becomes a transforming power and presence. In this love, there can be no defeat, only victory in the God who casts out all enemies.

Victory over Fear

Zephaniah's third affirmation concerns the most insidious enemy of all—the one that caused Israel so much trouble in the past: fear. When the God who renews us in love is in our midst, we have no reason to be afraid. Fear arises from the unknown. It is often based on false assumptions, on interpretations of reality that have no foundation in fact. This is what brought pain and embarrassment to Israel in the first place. The nation fell into sin because its people feared that God no longer cared about them, that they were missing life in its fullness by remaining faithful.

Zephaniah wrote the third chapter of his prophecy to correct their distorted thinking. No matter what the objective facts of a situation may suggest, God does not abandon people. No unknown exists here. God remains always faithful. This is true in every circumstance and for all time; therefore, there can be no fear.

Zephaniah's conclusions speak powerfully to Christians living in the final decade of the twentieth century. Fear could well be our supreme nemesis. It fuels the fires of hatred and greed, violence and oppression. As much as any other factor, fear sustains apartheid in South Africa, inspires terrorism and war in the Middle East, stalls the struggle for democracy in Eastern Europe and the Third World, and stymies U.S./Soviet relations.

Fear is as much an orientation as it is an emotion. It undermines trust and causes tension in relationships, whether between individuals or groups. Rather than enhancing mutuality, which in turn fosters personal and social wholeness, fear gives rise to a survival mentality, an obsessive need to feel secure. The many crises of these times, from the abuse of the biosphere to the national debt, from the breakdown of the family to the rise of violent crime, have intensified this emphasis on survival.

Survivalism creates an atmosphere of suspicion, an environment in which vulnerability becomes the order of the day. The United States may be the most powerful country on earth, but fear walks tall in the land. We have become a nation of strangers, distracted from without by growing threats to our welfare, disturbed from within by feelings of aloneness and insignificance, uncertainty and alienation.

Fear poses a threat not only to our well-being, but to our way of life as well. Fearful people are anxious people, unable to love or hope, persevere or risk, and therefore incapable of facing complex social and personal dilemmas with courage and faith.

But into our present circumstances comes the message of Zephaniah, who wrote, "The King of Israel, the LORD, is in your midst; / you shall fear disaster no more."

The reason we need not fear is found in the meaning of Advent. This season bears witness to the Christ, who enters every environment of fear to make faint hearts brave. The beginning of the Christian year celebrates this entry. It gathers up all of time and eternity and telescopes their meaning into a single and unrepeatable moment, the moment of the Lord's appearing, first as Bethlehem's babe, but eventually as Calvary's suffering servant and heaven's risen and conquering king.

Jesus comes to show that faith dispels fear. He comes to proclaim that life is more spiritual and moral than it is material. He enters the human experience to teach that selfishness causes anxiety, that only those who lose their lives for his sake will find them. His kingdom ensures fear's final demise. Though invisible, his kingdom undergirds all things, a bulwark against evil and a sign of the coming age of peace.

Advent is to Christmas what history is to the kingdom of God: It is a prelude to the revelation of divinity in its fullness. Advent calls us to embrace the only kind of faith that drives out fear, the faith of Jesus Christ. No amount of social change, worldly crisis, or personal tragedy can obscure the season's meaning. Like yeast leavening rising dough, or a mustard seed growing in fertile soil, Advent fulfills its purpose quietly but with powerful effect.

Advent dramatizes God's self-giving. In Jesus of Nazareth, God became weak and vulnerable in order to awaken the world to the romance of the kingdom of heaven. As people respond in faith, they discover the security of divine love, in which there is no fear. Reconciled to God and to each other, they become part of the new humanity in Christ. No longer alone, they can face every circumstance with courage.

Such is Zephaniah's word of hope. Daring without being naive, it derives its power from the eternal grace and truth that make the Christmas birth a liberating event for all time. Every dream of new life that has ever been dreamed, every vision of fulfillment that has ever been inspired, has sprung from this inexhaustible source of spiritual romance. The source of this romance is the Lord God Omnipotent, who grants hope to people as they endure the trials of today by trusting in the victory of tomorrow. To embrace this hope is to sound the death knell for defeat. It is to receive the gift of courage.

Prayer for the Third Sunday in Advent

O Thou who art so far beyond us yet so close beside us,
seldom do we transcend the tension of being so
near to you yet so distant from you.
We long for a complete and perfect redemption that will
unify the whole of who we are with the whole
of who you are.

We come to you, holy God, in the hope of finding in the
invisible world of the spirit, clear and certain
guidance for the visible world of everyday
affairs.
You invite us into your presence and do not turn us away.
You promise that
those who seek will find,
those who ask will receive,
those who knock will have the door opened to
them.
For these assurances, we offer our thanks.

As the season of Advent brings the shortening of days and
the early descent of darkness, we also confront
our fears.
We cannot control the world around us, nor is the world
within us always secure.
There are anxieties that trouble our minds, regrets that
haunt our consciences, hurts that burden our
hearts.
Without the courage that comes from hope, we would be
lost, dear God.
As we approach the Savior's manger this year, we pray
for this courage anew.

Help us remember that Jesus came
　　to take our sides,
　　　to bear our burdens,
　　　　to bind up our broken hearts.
Enable us so to trust in him that our minds might find
　　　　peace, our bodies, rest, and our spirits, freedom.
If you find anything in us that offends your holiness,
　　　cast it out, we pray.

Remind us of the eternal truths that, in beauty and
　　　simplicity, first gained access to our inner spirits
　　　and made us new people in Christ.
Awaken us to the joy of forgiveness and the possibility of
　　　renewal.

May your gift of courage lead us to accept ourselves for
　　　who and what we are without inflating our
　　　self-importance or deflating our self-worth.

Lead us upward to the the higher ground of transformed
　　　attitudes and sacrificial service.
Having called us to yourself in Christ, complete in us the
　　　work of new creation that you have begun.
　　　And prepare us to greet the day of his birth
　　　as the reconciled, healed, forgiven people you
　　　call us to be. AMEN.

Questions for Reflection and Study

1. The Scriptures suggest that it takes as much courage to believe as it does to love. This is amply illustrated in the stories of people such as Abraham and Moses, Ruth and Esther, Jeremiah and Daniel, Elizabeth and Mary, the women at the empty tomb, and the disciples in their missionary endeavors. Is it possible to be a passive Christian, or does faith demand a willingness to dare? How is the element of daring present in the Christmas event?

2. Read James 2:14-26 and reflect on the meaning of courage for a Christian. What does courage require? How does one obtain it if it is absent?

3. The reality of human fear is present in the Christmas story as the angels appear to the shepherds in the fields. Why were the shepherds afraid and how did they cope with their fear? Does their experience have relevance for modern people? If so, how?

4. There are many instances in the Bible in which people are exhorted to be courageous, but there are also examples of experiences in which people learn to accept their weaknesses and fears. Compare Joshua 1:1-9 with 2 Corinthians 12:5-10 (see also Matthew 26:36-46 and 69-75) and discuss the human problem of strength and weakness. Is it possible to resolve the tension between the need to be strong and the tendency to be weak? How does Advent address this tension?

5. Zephaniah 3:14-17 illustrates God's grace in delivering people from judgment and renewing them in love.

The theme of grace is also emphasized in John 1 as a major component of the incarnation's meaning. How is grace present in the Christmas story? What are some concrete ways in which we can become more aware of grace and be more responsive to it? Discuss grace as a major theme in religion. How does the teaching of Christianity on this subject differ from that of other religious traditions?

6. This chapter suggests that God's hiddenness is a major cause of conflict in our relationship to God. Do you agree or disagree? What are some ways in which this conflict is expressed and what might we do to address the problem?

7. Reflect upon the overall theme of this chapter, discussing the term "death knell" and its application to the life of faith. How can we understand the "already/not yet" character of this phrase as related to such things as judgment, evil enemies, fear, and defeat? Just because Advent has sounded the "death knell" for these adversaries, does that mean the battle is over? If not, what are the weapons of our warfare, and how might the sounding of the "death knell" influence how we approach the fight?

four

O Bethlehem!

Now you are walled around with a wall;
 siege is laid against us;
with a rod they strike the ruler of Israel
 upon the cheek.

But you, O Bethlehem of Ephrathah,
 who are one of the little clans of Judah,
from you shall come forth for me
 one who is to rule in Israel,
whose origin is from of old,
 from ancient days.
Therefore he shall give them up until the time
 when she who is in labor has brought forth;
then the rest of his kindred shall return
 to the people of Israel.
And he shall stand and feed his flock in the
 strength of the LORD,
 in the majesty of the name of the LORD his
 God.
And they shall live secure, for now he shall be
 great
 to the ends of the earth.

—Micah 5:1-4

Romance is an experience of heart, but also of place—the place of the first meeting, the special memory, the transforming intimacy. Perhaps it is a park where lovers walk, an airport that brings them together after a long separation, or a church where they commit themselves to each other in marriage. Such places become as much a part of a relationship as the lovers themselves. Though the power of a place may be subtle, it is undeniable. One need only consider the Christmas story to confirm this truth.

Christmas was on the mind of a young American clergyman as he approached Bethlehem on horseback on Christmas Eve in 1865. In the fading light of the early evening, he paused just beyond the city's borders to watch from the hills. The scene moved him deeply. He saw Bethlehem's narrow streets lined with modest homes. He thought about the people who lived there and how they depended on the land and their flocks for survival. He also pondered a mystery: In this city, the Savior of the world was born. In the stillness of that moment, Bethlehem became more than just another town; it became a place of romance.

Later that night, the young man worshiped at the Church of the Nativity, which some believe stands on the place where Christ was born. Before retiring for the evening, he wrote in his journal, "It seemed as if I could hear voices that I knew well, telling each other of the 'Wonderful Night.'" Three years later, in preparing for Christmas services at his church in Philadelphia, the young clergyman recaptured what he had felt on Christmas Eve in the Holy Land by writing a hymn.

His name was Phillips Brooks, and his hymn was "O Little Town of Bethlehem." Brooks would go on to serve as minister of Trinity Church in Boston for more than twenty years, but the message of his famous hymn continues to inspire Christians all over the world to this day.

O little town of Bethlehem,
How still we see thee lie!
Above thy deep and dreamless sleep
The silent stars go by.
Yet in thy dark streets shineth
The everlasting Light;
The hopes and fears of all the years
Are met in thee tonight.

Of Roots and Reversals

In all of history, there has never been a town like Bethlehem. Bethlehem is more than a place on a map; it is an ideal of the imagination, a dream of enchantment hidden in the heart. Even if we have never visited Bethlehem, it has visited us. Every year, for as far back as we can remember, its borders have intersected our lives, and its ancient residents have become our neighbors.

We have become intimately acquainted with an innkeeper who earned his living there, with shepherds who watched their flocks in the nearby fields, and with Magi who came from afar. Bethlehem is as much our town as it was theirs. It is the location of our spiritual roots, because the Christian faith first became possible there—there in the entry of a living, breathing Savior into the world.

Bethlehem is not just a city, but a symbol of peace. It is the place where the romance of the manger began as a spark and became a flame. Years earlier, a prophet named Micah knew it would be that way. Eight centuries before a manger became a cradle for divinity, Micah looked down the corridor of history and predicted it. Speaking with the voice of God, he said,

But you, O Bethlehem of Ephrathah,
who are one of the little clans
of Judah,

from you shall come forth for me
one who is to rule in Israel,
whose origin is from of old,
from ancient days.

—Micah 5:2

Micah carried on a tradition that had begun long before him. Bethlehem had been special to the Hebrew people for centuries because David had been born and anointed king there. His ancestors Ruth and Boaz had been married in Bethlehem, and Jacob's beloved wife Rachel was buried there. In biblical times, this city, surrounded by the "Ephrathah," the fruitful fields, had a special place in many hearts, just as it does today.

Bethlehem is special because it reminds the world of the great reversal contained in the gospel. Its prominence in the Christmas story emphasizes God's exalting of the humble and humbling of the exalted. Even more, Bethlehem symbolizes God's unconditional love for the lowly, God's quiet but persistent work of unifying all things in Christ and so bringing peace.

The gospel is a drama of contradiction that was first staged at Bethlehem. The drama's theme of romance can hardly be detected in the air of hostility and conflict that hangs heavy over today's world. Its message of gentleness rarely penetrates ears so accustomed to sounds of violence, nor does its vision of wholeness seem believable to eyes that see so much brokenness.

But the message and the vision persist. The gospel is about the power of powerlessness. It is about the riches of poverty, the holiness of the ordinary, the wisdom of foolishness. In the birth of Jesus, divinity and humanity became one. The first Christmas witnessed the accomplishment of the impossible: Mortal flesh and immortal Spirit met perfectly in a single human being.

Heaven and earth came together in Bethlehem's

manger, and they can never again be separated. It is all so extraordinary that it defies the mind's ability to understand it. The mind has no alternative but to join in a spiritual offering of spontaneous praise to God. Such is the effect of romance. The magic of its mystery elicits a joyous response, particularly when the romance comes as a free gift of God's grace, unexpected and irresistible, a dream fulfilled yet ever renewed to be dreamed again.

It all began in a specific place. The gospel had to become real somewhere before it could become real everywhere. That Jesus' birth happened at Bethlehem confirms that God's ways are not our ways, nor God's thoughts our thoughts. It would seem that Jerusalem would have been a much better stage for the gospel drama, or Rome, perhaps. These cities could boast of impressive buildings and distinguished citizens, of thriving businesses and fashionable neighborhoods; Bethlehem could not.

If it is true, as Pascal wrote in *Pensées,* that "nothing is thoroughly approved but mediocrity," Bethlehem deserved much approval in the ancient world. It was an insignificant place, a thoroughly mediocre village. At the time of Jesus' birth, Bethlehem looked like hundreds of other villages that dotted the landscape of Palestine. The desert of Judah provided an ominous backdrop for the two fertile hills on which the city was built. Bethlehem had little industry or commerce. It was small and old and poor, the opposite of everything we want to be.

Yet God chose this insignificant little town as the birthplace of the Christ. Out of weakness came strength. Out of obscurity came royalty. Out of a history of struggle came the possiblity of peace for the nations. Perhaps these truths have something to say to us. The romance of the manger enables us to see Bethlehem from a new perspective. It prods us to recognize qualities in this ancient city that could bring positive change to our lives.

Contrasts That Provide Alternatives

First-century Bethlehem had character. It had the kind of identity that can suggest refreshing alternatives to some of today's flawed values. For instance, this is the age in which bigger is considered better. People seek bigger successes in hopes that they will lead to a bigger reputation, a bigger salary, a bigger home, a bigger thrill. Bethlehem challenges this idea. Its prominence in the Christmas story suggests that small can be beautiful, that it takes maturity and discipline to live within boundaries, and that being more, not having more, should be our highest goal.

The modern age has also made an idol of youth. We fear growing old because we fear death. Our faith is not strong enough to embolden us against the indignities of the aging process and the inevitability of the grave. So we shun the elderly. They make us feel uncomfortable because they remind us of what we fear most. But in avoiding contact with older people, we sacrifice the opportunity to benefit from their wisdom and experience. Content with such a sacrifice, we invest in schemes to keep ourselves looking and feeling young, sometimes to our own embarrassment.

Recently scientists discovered that injections of a naturally occuring substance called human growth hormone (HGH) can make a person look up to twenty years younger. The catch is that the injections cost $14,000 for a year's supply! As Andrea Dorfman states in reporting on this development, "From the fruitless quest for the legendary Fountain of Youth to the current popularity of plastic surgery and Retin-A face cream, the search for ways to erase the sags and wrinkles of aging has never stopped."[1]

Bethlehem declares to the modern world that aging can occur with dignity and grace. As old as it was, Bethlehem became the setting for a romance. This fact reveals the inherent dignity of giving and receiving love, no matter what the age of the people involved. The secret of staying young will not be found in any scientific discovery, but in the power of love to renew a life.

Another value that Bethlehem's presence in the Christmas story challenges is the need to be strong. Sometimes this need originates within ourselves; at other times it arises in response to the expectations of others. A woman in my congregation cared for her invalid mother for seven years. This included turning her in her bed every two hours around the clock. Finally the mother died. Several days after the funeral was over and the rest of the family had gone home, I called the woman to see how she was. She said she was fine, but the one thing she couldn't understand was why she felt so exhausted.

The answer seemed obvious to me. She had drawn upon her inner reserves of strength for so long in meeting her mother's needs that at the end of seven years, she had no reserves left. As soon as her mother died, she allowed herself to do what she had felt like doing for some time— she collapsed.

In a less dramatic way, life puts all of us in a similar position. Our role as worker or student, taxpayer or commuter, spouse or parent demands more of us than we can deliver. In the face of such demands, we feel inwardly weak but must appear outwardly strong in order to maintain our self-respect and win the approval of others.

The environments in which most Americans live and work have become so competitive that to admit weakness is to court disaster. Signs of inadequacy or self-doubt can mean the end of a career or a relationship. No wonder America's number-one-selling prescription drug in recent years has been Zantac, an ulcer medication.

When I think of how essential it has become to appear strong in today's world, I am reminded of the comment of Lou Holtz, the head football coach at Notre

Dame University. A reporter asked him if his team's next game was a matter of life and death. "Oh no!" said Holtz. "It's much more important than that!" Some people attach similar importance to appearing strong and "in control," even at the cost of their own health.

How comforting to find Bethlehem, a symbol of weakness, at the heart of the Christmas story. Here is an affirmation that God helps those who *cannot* help themselves. No matter how strong we are, we break down at times. When the stress of work and family defeats us, we lose our ability to remain poised under pressure. We encounter grief over our personal losses. Anxieties and conflicts weigh heavily on our minds. We experience daily strain living in such an uncertain age, an age riddled with social injustice and economic upheaval, with political in-fighting and military posturing.

Bethlehem's weakness may seem irrelevant amidst all of this, but it is not. The city's part in the Christmas romance says that God's visitation comes when problems are bigger than anyone can handle. Bethlehem bears witness that something good can emerge out of weakness, that God's surprises happen when least expected. If hope can be revealed in a manger in a town like Bethlehem, it can be revealed in us as well. Because of Christmas, hope meets us not only when we are on top and in control, but also when we feel beaten and helpless, overwhelmed by life and on the verge of collapse.

The Peace That Hope Brings

Bethlehem's testimony has endured across the centuries. As we struggle to find purpose in our restless striving and frenzied busyness, the city confronts us with our misplaced priorities. We invest much in trying to find ourselves, but here is a town whose only claim to fame is that it was found by God. We spend our lives searching for that special place where we feel at home. We long to say what Isak Dinesen says in her book *Out of Africa* about waking each morning on her farm at the foot of the Ngong Hills and thinking to herself, "Here I am, where I ought to be." We feel that in finding such a place, a place "where we ought to be," we would also find ourselves. But the Bethlehem motif of the Christmas drama suggests otherwise. Not in finding, but in being found, do we discover God's peace.

To borrow Isaiah's image, every valley was lifted up, and every hill and mountain brought low; the crooked places were made straight, and the rough places a plain, that God's glory could be revealed in Bethlehem's manger and believing hearts could sing,

> For Christ is born of Mary,
> And gathered all above,
> While mortals sleep, the angels keep
> Their watch of wondering love.
> O morning stars, together
> Proclaim the holy birth!
> And praises sing to God the King,
> And peace to all on earth.

There was openness in Bethlehem's character, an openness that forged the best possibilities out of the worst circumstances. For a brief, shining moment Bethlehem embodied the scandal of the gospel. God's revelation appeared not in Herod's palace, not in Rome's corridors of power, or Jerusalem's sacred temple, but in Bethlehem's lowliest accommodations, out behind the overcrowded inn, out where a dark and dirty stable provided animals a refuge from the cold.

There were not many places in town that welcomed the Christmas child; what matters is that one place did. Because of that stable, Bethlehem, whose name means "House of Bread," had as its guest the One who is the Bread of Life for the world, and whoever eats of this Bread will live.

Bethlehem made room for Christ's birth and so received his peace. As Edmund Steimle has noted, Christmas is the calm at the eye of the storm, a moment of tranquility in the long night of the world's turbulence. Christmas invites us not into sentimental escapism, but into rugged, realistic faith. The Prince of Peace came to an occupied city. Bethlehem knew the tension of the Roman presence, with its oppressive tax demands and its armies poised for a fight. The peace of Christ's birth came amidst all of the deprivation, anger, and uncertainty of the time, and so it comes today. A report from Bethlehem that appeared in the *New York Times* on Christmas Day in 1989 stresses the point:

> For a third successive year, Christmas came without joy to those who live here, the town's shrines ringed by soldiers and the season's supposed good will all but extinguished by conflict between Arab and Jew. . . .
>
> In Manger Square, soldiers blocked all entrance streets, body-searched pilgrims and rummaged through bags. Throughout Christmas Eve, Bethlehem had been closed by a commercial strike called by the underground leadership of the uprising that left the stores hidden by cream-painted shutters.[2]

Christ's birth heralded the peace for which all of life longs. The birth did not happen in a fantasyland of artificial serenity, but in the real world's crucible of tension and turmoil. In a sense, the Bethlehem of the first century was no different from the Bethlehem of today. It was a town in which fallible people tried to find meaning and security amidst ominous circumstances.

The peace that came to them through the Christmas message was not a Pollyanna peace; it did not deny the tragedy inherent in their lives or in life itself. It was the peace that hope brings. This peace resides at the heart of all things but is presently obscured by evil. Christmas established a beachhead for peace on the shores of human despair. As Phillips Brooks wrote,

> How silently, how silently
> The wondrous gift is given!
> So God imparts to human hearts
> The blessings of His heaven.
> No ear may hear His coming,
> But in this world of sin,
> Where meek souls will receive Him, still
> The dear Christ enters in.

Now peace can be found even amidst the most extreme conditions. However tentative and fragmentary its presence may be, peace is here to stay. Wherever it emerges, whether between nations or persons or in the interminable restlessness of the human heart, it is a sign of things to come.

Christmas reminds the world of its higher destiny, the destiny that will be realized in the fullness of time when Christ's peace reigns in all the earth. Bethlehem is a witness of this peace. It calls us to practice the disciplines of patient waiting and endurance. These disciplines have been part of the city's identity for centuries. In them, the hope is renewed that today's faint glimmers of fragile human peace will soon be transformed into the eternal and invincible peace of God, which passes all understanding.

O Bethlehem! May God help us remember the peace revealed in you on the night when Christ was born. When we lose our way, or when the path toward understanding is obstructed by insurmountable barriers, bring us back to him who came not to condemn but to save. In the romance of his love, may our peace be found.

Prayer for the Fourth Sunday in Advent

God of all people and all places, we draw near to you
    because you have first drawn near to us.
We come expectantly, seeking a glimpse of your glory in
    Bethlehem's manger.
We come with reverence, humbling ourselves in the
    presence of your holiness.
We approach you just as we are, with all of our burdens
    and thanksgivings, our fears and possibilities,
    our griefs and joys.

In Christ you have become for us the Bread of Life, the
    One who satisfies our hungering souls with the
    truth of your Word and nourishes our rising
    hopes with the power of your presence.
We are sustained by your grace, O God.
Because of the gift of your Son's coming, there is
    no distance far enough,
        no obstacle great enough,
            no problem insurmountable enough to separate us
            from you.
For this, we give thanks.

You do not force us to acknowledge you as Lord, but you
    have created us in such a way that we cannot be
    whole until we do.
In fellowship with your Spirit and your people, we
    discover the deeper truth of our time and place
    on earth—
the truth that we are not our own, that we are part
    of you, as you are part of us.

Bring us back to Bethlehem, O God, that we might find
    the roots of our faith.

Amidst the stresses and uncertainties of our lives, lead us
to the manger, that we might rejoice with those
who first welcomed the infant Christ.
Help us look for you not just in places and among people
where we would expect to find you, but also
where your presence takes us by surprise and
forces us to reexamine our values and faith.

Make us aware of the uncommon joy to be found in the
commonness of routine activities.
Help us to see possibilities in situations that seem
impossible.
In our moments of weakness, teach us not to quit, but to
trust.
Still the panic that arises within us when our trials
overshadow our triumphs.

Attune our hearts to the voice of your Spirit, which is
constantly speaking words of peace.
Give us ears to hear, that our outward actions may reflect
the inward calm that comes as a gift of your
presence.
And remind us that we can never stray so far that you
cannot find us and bring us back home again.
AMEN.

Questions for Reflection and Study

1. This chapter has emphasized the importance of Bethlehem as a place of God's revelation. This emphasis coincides with the Bible's consistent attention to where significant events happen, particularly events related to the salvation history of the community of faith. God's revelation comes in secular places as well as sacred ones. Reflect upon which of these places of revelation, if either, is more prominent in Scripture. For instance, compare 1 Samuel 3:1-18 with Genesis 3:1-15, and Deuteronomy 12:1-15 with Acts 9:1-9.

   Contrast the way God's revelation came to people in such places as deserts, mountains, and various working environments (such as the seashore), with the way God's revelation came in the temple and other religious contexts. In the Bible, where does God speak most often, in religious or secular places, or both? What is God's purpose in each? Does the context sometimes change the purpose?

2. Is it possible for the sacred to be profane and the profane to be sacred at times? If so, what are the dangers of this possibility? (Consider, for instance, the conflicts caused in the Holy Land when different religions claim the same places as sacred). Specifically, what makes a certain place either sacred or profane? Does God honor these distinctions, or are they human inventions? Give examples from the Bible to support your answer.

   A corollary question: Is it just as likely that a person will encounter God in nature as in church? How does the Christmas event, and the role of Bethlehem in it, influence your response?

3. It is a fact that relationships always happen somewhere. Whether they are beginning or ending, growing or stagnating, they have as their context the specific places where people live their lives. How small or large a role does a particular context play in determining the quality of relationships? How much does our awareness of where we are affect our understanding of who we are? What do our memories of special times spent with another person in a certain place communicate to us about the nature of God and the human condition? Think about the places of Christmas such as Bethlehem, the inn, the stable, and the manger. Do they tell us anything about God's character and God's message for humanity?

4. The stories of Advent and Christmas are about aging as well as birth. John the Baptist was born to aged parents, Zechariah and Elizabeth; Jesus was born in Bethlehem, an ancient city; he was also blessed in the temple by Simeon and Anna, both of whom were advanced in years. What does this say about the continuity of the human life cycle? In what ways might the Christmas event strengthen and inform the Bible's teaching about reverence for the elderly? (See Leviticus 19:32; Job 32:6; Proverbs 16:31; 20:29; 23:22; and 1 Timothy 5:1-2).

5. Bethlehem functions in the Christmas story as a metaphor for the potential of weakness. This theme is also suggested in the entry of a helpless baby into the world. Christianity is sometimes criticized as a religion of the weak (by the philosopher Friedrich Nietzsche, for instance). Is this fair? Does the New Testament

support this view? Can you think of instances in which strength can be a weakness and weakness can be a strength? Refer to 2 Corinthians 12:7-10 in responding to these questions.

6. Bethlehem's role in the events of Christmas raises the question of whether we "find" God or God "finds" us. What is the emphasis of the birth narratives of the Gospels on this matter? (Consider, for instance, the experience of Mary and Elizabeth). How might an understanding of God as the One who initiates relationship with us, rather than us with God, affect our spiritual life? Should this matter be seen as an either/or or a both/and?

---

[1]Andrea Dorfman, "Getting a Shot of Youth," *Time*, July 16, 1990, pp. 54-55.

[2]Alan Cowell, "Peace in Bethlehem, Little Good Will," *New York Times*, December 25, 1989, p. 3.

five

*Majesty
in a
Manger*

In those days a decree went out from Caesar Augustus
that all the world should be enrolled. This was the first enroll-
ment, when Quirinius was governor of Syria. And all went to
be enrolled, each to his own city. And Joseph also went up
from Galilee, from the city of Nazareth, to Judea, to the city of
David, which is called Bethlehem, because he was of the house
and lineage of David, to be enrolled with Mary, his betrothed,
who was with child. And while they were there, the time came
for her to be delivered. And she gave birth to her first-born son
and wrapped him in swaddling cloths, and laid him in a
manger, because there was no place for them in the inn.

—*Luke 2:1-14, RSV*

Arlene Croce, a well-known commentator on the arts in New York City, once wrote of the celebrated ballerina Suzanne Farrell that she was "always off balance and always secure." Croce's words describe a fundamental paradox. It would seem impossible to be off balance and secure at the same time, but the genius of a great ballerina transcends impossibility. Her dancing holds in tension the opposing impulses of daring and reticence, of recklessness and caution. What emerges is a performance of such grace and brilliance that it can only be called a miracle, a wonder of creative movement and beauty.

Romance, like art, also contains elements of paradox. It can inspire or confound, enliven or disturb. When most expected to succeed, it fails; when most expected to fail, it succeeds. At its best, romance gives rise to chivalry and creativity, to compassion and courage; at its worst, it fuels the fires of jealousy, rage, and violence. Romance gave the world the sonnets of Shakespeare and Elizabeth Barrett Browning; it also led Dr. Faust to sell his soul to the devil, and Herod to keep his promise to Salome by having John the Baptist beheaded.

Romance defies explanation. It can lift the human spirit to majestic heights of joy or plunge it to dark depths of despair. It is a fickle phenomenon. If you go out looking for it, romance will elude you. If you sit back and wait for it, it will mock and tantalize you. It inflames the heart at the most inconvenient times, like when you are already attached, when you are preoccupied with other pursuits, or when there's little or no chance that your love will be returned. But once romance casts its spell, it commands awesome power, for well or ill, in a life. Its presence makes all the world look bright; its absence dims that brightness, making an already forbidding landscape more forbidding still.

The Manger and Its Critics

As noted in chapter one, Christmas confronts us with a similar paradox. A basic incongruity lies at the heart of this day. The incongruity can become a possibility, as Reinhold Niebuhr suggested, but only through faith. Christ's coming brought joy, but the joy was revealed in a joyless world, a world broken by sin and all of its poverty and war, violence and oppression, pain and injustice. A predictable response to Christmas is that it's too good to be true. The idea of perfect love being revealed in an imperfect world strikes a discordant note in many modern minds.

We are too accustomed to the real world's unforgiving laws of nature and its "survival of the fittest" ethic to accept the Christmas miracle at face value. Like the character Hazel Mote in one of Flannery O'Connor's stories, we expect the world to be a place "where the blind don't see and the lame don't walk and what's dead stays that way."[1] The miracle of God becoming man in Jesus Christ seems unbelievable because it suggests a fundamental contradiction, a deviation from the status quo.

Can the almighty Creator of the heavens and earth take on human form? Can an infinite Spirit inhabit a finite body? It seems impossible. The sense of impossiblity intensifies when we think long and hard about the world. True, sometimes the sun shines brilliantly in this world; sometimes people transcend their personal differences to accomplish noble goals together; sometimes children laugh, and young people fall in love, and friends and family sit down for a meal with warmth in their hearts and words of celebration on their lips. Sometimes the world is a beautiful place.

But too often the beauty is obscured by ugliness. A drug-dependent mother gives birth to an addicted infant. A homeless man huddles next to a steam grate, fighting a losing battle against the frigid cold. A home is robbed, a woman raped, a child abused. Looking gaunt and haggard, a person with AIDS grimaces in pain, cursing the unfairness of the disease. A nursing home resident dies alone, finally humbled by the indignities of life's sunset years. This, too, happens in the world.

Some years ago, when John G. Winant, one of Britain's most beloved diplomats, committed suicide, his death was regarded a tragic loss in the United States as well as England. In the wake of the tragedy, the *Manchester Guardian* carried an editorial that captured the agonizing incongruity of the random intermingling of good and evil in life. The editorial said, "It is a sad commentary on our postwar world that John Winant could not bear to live in it."[2]

In light of such harsh realities, it is inevitable that cynicism would gain a foothold in the human heart. It seems naive to believe in the ultimate triumph of right over wrong when wrong seems so invincible at present. That triumph may come in fairy tales or in a Pollyanna optimist's daydreams, but in the real world it seldom does.

The paradox of evil's consistent thwarting of good remains unresolved. For some people this means faith is so much foolishness. Who would be gullible enough to believe in a just and loving God in a world in which injustice and hate abound? What would lead someone to commit such a blatant crime against reason?

Some contend that these times call for uncompromising skepticism. God is a crutch, they say. The spiritual quest only diverts attention from the search for real answers to painfully real problems. No wonder William F. Buckley, Jr., would say to Malcolm Muggeridge in a television interview, "If you mention God more than once at a dinner party, you aren't invited back."

Yet beneath the doubts and questions that haunt the modern consciousness lies an indomitable religious spirit. Surveys have consistently shown that over 90 percent of the American people believe in God. In spite of skepticism's seductive appeal, we still seek an answer to the paradox created by the clash of evil with good.

But our best intellectual arguments leave us cold. Our efforts to create a just society always fall short. Our faith in human ingenuity results in disappointment when the patient on the operating table dies, the jumbo jet crashes, or the computers fail and shut down the entire phone system. We don't have the answer to the tragic paradoxes of life; only God does. That is why Christmas brings the romance of hope to the world.

Transcending Absurdity and Obscenity

Christmas testifies that the heights and depths of human experience are part of the same sacred space and that God is Lord of all. To be sure, perplexing contrasts confront us on every side. The same person who in one moment experiences more joy than can be contained may, in the next, feel more grief than can possibly be borne. Some people suffer; others live in comfort and ease. For both of these experiences to be possible simultaneously would seem to reduce life to the level of absurdity, even obscenity. And without Christmas, that is where life would remain.

Without God's presence with us in Christ, you and I would be subjected to the terror of cosmic aloneness. The space we inhabit would not be sacred; it would be desolate. If we could talk about God at all, it would be only in speculative terms. Apart from Christmas, God would be nothing more than a theory, an abstraction without definition. Ideals such as love and justice and peace would remain only ideals, passionless and dead.

But hear again the good news that this day proclaims. We are told that the shepherds, "went with haste, and found Mary and Joseph, and the babe lying in a manger. And when they saw it they made known the saying which had been told them concerning this child; and all who heard it wondered" (Luke 2:16-18, RSV).

The message of Christmas is that God has entered all of the agonies and ecstasies of life. It took the incongruity of divinity and humanity bonding together perfectly in the Christ child to resolve the incongruity of joy and sorrow being equally present in human experience. In order for life to make sense, it first had to make room— room for the One who represents the best in us all. Because of him, life is not an absurdity or an obscenity; it's a testament of hope and a vessel of the holy.

That is why the shepherds, and everyone who heard about it, wondered. They had seen the simple and the profound in perfect harmony. History and eternity had suddenly intersected, and the result was majesty in a manger. Granted, there was a "sameness" about Jesus' birth; it took place like every other human birth. But it was different as well. It brought heaven down to earth and made it possible for earth to be lifted up to heaven.

The mystery of this birth is in a class by itself. Everyone understands it, yet no one understands it. Its simplicity warms the heart; its complexity baffles the mind. It is weakness and power simultaneously. It is greatness and insignificance in a single event. It is judgment and grace in unison, reality and fantasy all at once. It is all of these things because life is all of these things, and Christ was born to liberate and redeem all of life.

When we are confronted with majesty in a manger, we find ourselves suddenly short of breath. Kneeling becomes the only appropriate posture for body and soul. Words might suffice for some descriptions, but for this, only art will do. So paint the holy birth into a timeless portrait of color and light. Compose it into an exalted symphony. Write it into a majestic poem that brings renewed life to every generation. Translate it into a Gospel narrative at the hand of Luke, and send it across the centuries until it resounds in every believing heart on

Christmas morning, and until it says, "For to you is born this day in the city of David a Savior, who is Christ the Lord" (Luke 2:11, RSV).

Marveling at the Wonder of Perfect Love

Christmas introduced a unifying theme into the explosion of clashing colors and conflicting sounds that is life. The unifying theme is love, and when the power of its romance captivates the human heart, it inspires wonder within. Such is the effect of an illuminating encounter with majesty in a manger. One can only pause to hear the harmony of its music and marvel at the symmetry of its design.

A famous photograph taken by Yousuf Karsh shows the renowned Spanish cellist Pablo Casals with his back to the camera. Karsh recalls that he was so moved as he listened from a distance to Casals playing Bach that he could not for some moments attend to photography. It seemed just right to pose Casals facing away from the camera.

It is said that years later, when the photograph was on exhibition at the Museum of Fine Arts in Boston, an elderly gentleman would come and stand for many minutes in front of it. Curious about this ritual, a curator finally asked, "Sir, why do you come here and stand in front of this picture?"

The curator was met with a withering glance and the rebuke, "Hush, young man. Can't you see? I'm listening to the music!"[3]

Christmas has a similar effect on all who open their hearts to its romance. No one understands it. All we can do is listen to its music. To encounter the majesty of God's glory in Bethlehem's manger is to be filled with awe. It is to pause in the stillness and worship him whose birth promises peace to the world. The paradox of God becoming man makes no sense; there is even a certain vulgarity to it all. That's why it is so scandalous, yet so wonderful. Frederick Buechner recognizes this when he exclaims:

> The vulgarity of a God who adorns the sky at sunrise and sundown with colors no decent painter would dream of placing together on a single canvas, the vulgarity of a God who created a world full of hybrids like us—half ape, half human—and who keeps breaking back into the muck of this world. The vulgarity of a God who was born into a cave among hicks and the steaming dung of beasts only to grow up and die on a cross between crooks.[4]

Here again is the paradox of the gospel. What seems vulgar to us is holy to God. Because of Christ's coming, the space we inhabit is now always and forever sacred, and nothing—absolutely nothing—can change that. No disaster is so tragic that it can shut out God's presence. No war is so terrible that hope cannot arise from the ashes. No personal crisis is so irredeemable that something good cannot be salvaged from it. Now, in all these things, we are more than conquerors through him who loved us.

This is the meaning of Christmas. The holy child of Bethlehem disarmed life's tension at its source. Majesty in a manger was not an afterthought, but a necessity. We do not have enough light within us to dispel the darkness in the world. We do not know enough of the truth to counter all of the lies. Our perceptions of the holy are too flawed and limited to transform the unholy places of life into what they should be.

We need someone to help us, and that is why Christ was born. Before the foundation of the world, God knew we would not be able to save ourselves. God knew that the salvation of our race would require the ultimate sacrifice, the sending of God's own Son.

Many stories by the Italian writer Primo Levi explore the question of human vulnerability. One story in particular may hold a clue to how vulnerable the cosmic Christ must have felt on his way to becoming Mary's son, the Jesus of history. Levi tells of an unborn soul who is offered the opportunity to be born as a healthy, privileged, white male whose life will not only be free from want, but will also contribute powerfully to the alleviation of human suffering. Instead, the soul chooses to be born like everyone else, at random, in order to make his own way in the world, whatever the risks.[5]

Jesus made a similar choice in entering our time and space at Christmas. He freely subjected himself to the isolation and pain, the coldness and cruelty of the human condition in order to bring the romance of hope to us all. What we had to offer him was a manger. The manger represents our attempt to give him a place in a world that needs him so desperately but does not know how to welcome him. The manger symbolizes our poverty, our embarrassment, our perplexity, in the presence of God. We know we need God's presence in our lives, but we are not sure we want it. It demands too much from us. It uncovers too many of our shortcomings and reveals too many of our sins.

But, welcome or not, God comes to the world in Christ and fills it with majesty. God takes what we have to offer, no matter how humble or common, and the offering assumes a life beyond itself. The manger proclaims that love and grace are at the center of reality and that one day all people will walk in the light of God's truth.

Something beautiful happened in Christ's birth, and no incident of ugliness can take the beauty away. Something joyful happened there, and no sorrow can stop the angels from singing. When God's majesty was revealed in the manger, everyone who heard about it wondered. They knew that life would be different, that this birth would give people new eyes with which to see and new ears with which to hear. Christmas invites us all to see and hear the romance of hope.

So come to the manger. Take the path that leads through the narrow streets and by the simple shops and homes. Keep following the path until it leads you to a noisy and crowded inn with no vacancies. But don't stop there. Follow farther, until you come to the stable out back where the animals are kept. Stay on the path until it takes you there. Don't be satisfied with any other path, any easier path. Keep following until you take your place with Mary and Joseph and the shepherds and the wise men.

Come as you are. Bring your emptiness and your fullness. Bring all of your conflict and all of your peace, all of your laughter and all of your tears, all of your hope and all of your despair. Bring the innumerable pieces of your life—those pieces that fit neatly together and those that never will—and present them as gifts to the Christ who was born there. Present them in the confidence that he will take all of the pieces of who you are and mold them into a new, unified whole. When you come to him, joining the others who are already there, you will encounter majesty in a manger. And it will fill your heart with wonder.

Prayer for Christmas

Majestic God, we greet the birth of Christ this day with
uplifted spirits and abiding joy.
We have heard the sound of the angels singing.
We have seen the star shining brightly in the heavens.
We have joined Mary and Joseph, the shepherds,
and the wise men in encountering the mystery
of the holy birth.
We have come to the manger and stood in the presence of
your glory, revealed in the Christmas child.

Your Spirit has borne witness, O God, that the glory of the
manger is
more real than all the wars that have ever been fought,
more enduring than all of the conflict and confusion
that have ever been known,
more tender than all of the tears that have ever been
wept.
We rejoice that your will was done in the holy birth, and
that you receive us as your children when we
respond to your love in faith.
We thank you that Christmas means more than an
opportunity to celebrate; it is the day on which
we are born in hope, and hope is born in us.

We approach the manger, O God, in the confidence that
life's incongruities find resolution there.
We come knowing that in Jesus you are present in our
every grief, our every doubt, our every fear.
Such knowledge fills us with wonder and praise.
We praise you for the message of the manger,
for the romance of hope that brings clarity to our
confusion and possibility to our perplexity.
Your gift to us of Christ is so extravagant that our only
appropriate response is to give ourselves to you
wholly in return.

In Christmas you bring us the miracle of your peace,
     O Lord, the peace that seems so far from the
     world of today, but will be realized fully in the
     new heaven and new earth of tomorrow.
Make room in our hearts for this peace, we pray.
Reveal yourself to us anew.
Cast out the despair we feel on gray winter days when the
     night falls so heavy that light seems forever
     gone.
Take us beyond the drudgery of our daily routine into the
     drama of liberating faith.

Drive away the weariness that assaults us when our
     struggles and anxieties seem more than we can
     bear.
Hold before us a vision of a life that is truly ours because it
     is fully yours.
Grant us glimpses of your glory, so brilliantly present in
     the newborn Christ, that our outward actions
     may reflect the inward wonder of your
     illuminating presence.
Fill us with the hope and joy of Christmas, that we may
     become instruments of your love, bringing
     healing to a broken world. AMEN.

Questions for Reflection and Study

1. In his book *Orthodoxy*, G.K. Chesterton makes the point that heresy results when people overemphasize one side of the gospel. Orthodoxy, on the other hand, always balances opposites against each other. This keeps them from splintering apart and aligns them with the underlying revelation of truth at the center of biblical faith. What opposites were brought into harmony by Christ's birth? Do you see these both in his nature and his message? In answering these questions, read the following verses: John 1:14; Matthew 10:16; Philippians 4:12; Romans 5:20; Romans 11:22; and 1 Corinthians 12:10. Also, compare Luke 14:28 with Matthew 6:34; and Matthew 25:30 with Luke 23:24.

2. In his book *Mere Christianity*, C.S. Lewis makes the following statement:

   Besides being complicated, reality, in my experience, is usually odd. It is not neat, not obvious, not what you expect. For instance, when you have grasped that the earth and the other planets all go round the sun, you would naturally expect that all the planets were made to match—all at equal distances from each other, say, or distances that regularly increased, or all the same size, or else getting bigger or smaller as you go farther from the sun. In fact, you find no rhyme or reason (that we can see) about either the sizes or the distances; and some of them have one moon, one has four, one has two, some have none, and one has a ring.

   Reality, in fact, is usually something you could not have guessed. That is one of the reasons I believe Christianity. It is a religion you could not have guessed.[6]

In light of Lewis's statement, reflect on the meaning of Christmas. Is God's coming as an infant in a manger something anyone would have expected? If not, is this a confirmation or denial of the truth of the gospel? Read 1 Corinthians 1:18-25: Would it be legitimate to substitute the word "manger" for "cross" in these verses? How would this substitution affect the meaning of these verses, if at all?

3. The Latin proverb *Nil credam et omnia cavebo* (Believe nothing and be on guard against everything) rings true for many people in modern America. But such skepticism deprives people of experiencing the joy of Christmas, since the very fact that you cannot explain Christ's birth is what makes it so wonderful. What role does an appreciation for mystery play in faith? If one loses this appreciation, is it still possible to believe? What are the similarities and differences between the mystery of human romance and divine love? Can you think of other interfaces between mysteries of life and mysteries of faith? How do we usually respond to them, and what lesson might there be in this for how we respond to Christmas?

4. Do you think that Christ's birth in a manger was coincidental, or was God making a statement by allowing him to be born there? Do the circumstances surrounding Christ's birth say anything about God's involvement in human struggle? What personal or social values might be inferred from the idea of majesty in a manger? How does this idea relate to God's concern for the poor or God's commitment to justice?

5. Frederick Buechner uses the word "vulgar" to describe Christ's birth. He does this to emphasize how offensive

and scandalous it is to think of God humbling himself in such a lowly way. Is "vulgar" an appropriate word in this context? How do you react to it? In light of the offense of Christmas, how do we make sense of the outpouring of sentimentality associated with the infant Jesus. In what ways, if at all, is this sentimentality dangerous, and how might it be counterbalanced by Buechner's emphasis?

[1]Quoted in Dan Wakefield, "And Now, a Word from Our Creator," *New York Times Book Review*, February 12, 1989, p. 28.

[2]Quoted in Gerald Kennedy, *The Lion and the Lamb* (Nashville: Abingdon-Cokesbury Press, 1950), p. 199.

[3]See "Personal Glimpses," *Reader's Digest*, November 1984, p. 169.

[4]Frederick Buechner, *The Hungering Dark* (San Francisco: Harper and Row Publishers, 1985), p. 67.

[5]See Primo Levi, *The Sixth Day and Other Stories*, trans. Raymond Rosenthal (New York: Summit Books, 1990).

[6]C.S. Lewis, *Mere Christianity* (New York: Macmillan Publishing Co., 1973), p. 47.

six

The Light in the Window

In the beginning was the Word, and the Word was with God, and the Word was God. He was in the beginning with God. All things came into being through him, and without him not one thing came into being. What has come into being in him was life, and the life was the light of all people. The light shines in the darkness, and the darkness did not overcome it.

There was a man sent from God, whose name was John. He came as a witness to testify to the light, so that all might believe through him. He himself was not the light, but he came to testify to the light. The true light, which enlightens everyone, was coming into the world.

He was in the world, and the world came into being through him; yet the world did not know him. He came to what was his own, and his own people did not accept him. But to all who received him, who believed in his name, he gave power to become children of God, who were born, not of blood or of the will of the flesh or of the will of man, but of God.

—John 1:1-18

Anyone who has ever been in love knows that romance fills life with light. Everything suddenly looks brighter. When someone you love returns your affection, your heart cannot be downcast; it brims with joy. Personal problems become manageable. Fears subside. Anxieties flee. People in love project a certain radiance. They inhabit a world of wonder.

I am not speaking here about the dreamy naiveté of star-crossed escapism, even less about the false euphoria of infatuation. I am talking about authentic mutuality in the context of intimacy. I am talking about two vulnerable human spirits bonding as one as they respond to God's gift of love, a gift made manifest in respect and self-giving, caring and commitment.

Before the gift can be received, potential lovers must discover each other. Romance must be given the chance to work its magic in their hearts. When the magic happens, light is often involved. A romance begins over a candlelight dinner in a nice restaurant or cozy apartment. The magic is initiated during a walk on the beach under a moonlit sky or in the depths of conversation in front of the fire. Whatever the context, romance sets life aglow; without it, darkness intrudes and hope falters.

The Drama Behind the Human Dilemma

The romance of light and hope is the theme of a story that may help illuminate the backdrop against which John wrote the prologue to his Gospel. As the story goes, an aspiring writer was given the opportunity to read his best piece of fiction to a very old and wise author. The plot involved the only son of a poor widow who lived in a little cottage nestled in a valley in Pennsylvania.

One day the son set out for New York City to seek his fortune. As he left, his mother took him aside and said to him, "Now remember, son, if you ever get into trouble, no matter how bad it is, you make your way back home, and as you come over the hill and look down into the valley, you will always find a light burning in this window—and I will be waiting to welcome you."

The young writer went on to describe what happened when the boy got to the big city. The description was tragic: The charms of New York's darker side proved too much to resist; the boy ended up in prison. Developing all of this in vivid detail, the young writer went on to tell how the boy was finally released and decided to make for home and mother.

The boy hitchhiked most of the way and finally got back to Pennsylvania. As he walked up over the crest of the hill that led down into the familiar valley where he had grown up, he saw the outline of his mother's old cottage in the evening twilight. His heart filled with hope. But to his bitter disappointment, there was no light burning in the window! At this point, the old author who had been listening to the story leapt to his feet and shouted at the young man who had written it, "You young upstart! PUT THAT LIGHT BACK!"[1]

Life without the romance of the manger is life in darkness. Without Christ, a light never shines in the window. In place of the light lurks a fathomless void, menacing and grim. The void greets the eyes of all who are weary and trying to make their way back home. Their anticipation turns to disappointment, their faith, to despair.

But God did not originally intend it to be that way. In the beginning, divine love radiated throughout the heavens. Love compelled God to create, to share the essence of the Creator's nature with other beings. God's romance with creation began when the earth was a formless void and darkness covered the face of the deep. God spoke and said, " 'Let there be light'; and there was light" (Genesis 1:3).

From that moment on, darkness was not meant to be a problem in any place or for any person. Human beings were put on earth to live in the light. They were meant to revel in the light's purity, frolic in its glow, and receive inspiration and life from its energy. But as time went on, they became fascinated with darkness instead. They found that they could hide in the darkness, that they could conceal their true motives in it and perform evil acts under the security of its cover.

Before long, the darkness, which God originally intended to be insignificant, became so prominent that it threatened to extinguish all light. The romance of hope lost its influence. Darkness began to expand its reign with such power that no one could contend with it. Soon the darkness encroached on the domain previously controlled by the light. In communities and groups, the light of cooperation became the darkness of dissension. In personal relationships, the light of understanding became the darkness of hostility. In the human heart, the light of love and generosity became the darkness of fear and selfishness.

But the first chapter of John's Gospel tells us that the Christmas event changed all of this. The birth of Jesus Christ was God's way of saying, "Put that light back! Put it back to testify that God's romance with humanity will never die. Put it back in the window for every returning prodigal to see. Put it back to say that someone's home and someone cares."

But not only that. "Put that light back so that it can dispel the darkness. Put it back so that the light's brilliance can shine out across the valley and up over the hill and on into the city, and from there, into every other city and town and neighborhood in the world, until every place on earth is illuminated by the magnificent, shining radiance of God's presence."

Throughout the Christmas season, the church declares that the light is with us in Jesus Christ. Now the romance of hope can flourish again. In John's words, "What has come into being in him was life, and the life was the light of all people. The light shines in the darkness, and the darkness did not overcome it" (John 1:3b-5).

No More Domination

Because of Christmas, there will always be a light in the window. It was put there by God and no power in all of creation can extinguish it. It is the light of Christ, a light signifying that no matter how dominating and intimidating and suffocating the darkness may seem, the darkness will not last forever—its days are numbered; its eventual demise certain.

The dominating presence of darkness is a concern for us all; it brings a feeling of gloom. Whether present in real circumstances or imagined perceptions, gloom stifles romance. An older woman discovered this as she reflected on her marriage of many years. "When I was a single girl," she said, "I promised myself I would never marry a man who was bald, wore glasses, or had artificial teeth. I didn't—but now he *is, does,* and *has!*"

Another woman was also disillusioned with her marriage. She let her feelings show when, with arms folded and a superior expression on her face, she said to her husband, "A good husband needs to be strong, caring, and sensitive. You have all but three of those qualities!"

Just as the darkness of negativity can ruin a relationship, so can physical darkness snuff out hope. In Jesus' day, the people feared that the world was coming to an end when the days grew short in December. With no electricity, they were forced to rely on oil-burning lamps and torches to see their way; they lived much of their lives fumbling and groping through the dark.

Darkness—the absence of light—represents chaos, a state of life marked by confusion and panic, even insanity. Love cannot grow in such a state; fear won't let it. As

John's words suggest, darkness is the domain of evil. Evil is not neutral; it possesses mighty, malevolent power and affects everyone. Even the most buoyant spirits submit to the destructive seductions of the dark. Because the darkness cannot be ignored, it must be fought with all one's might.

Some people consistently lose the battle. They have what psychologists call "seasonal affective disorder" (SAD). The disorder occurs when depression sets in as the result of deprivation of light. For many, Christmas is a depressing season. There has always been a close association between darkness and death; in late December, many people feel dead inside. The constant, unrelenting physical presence of darkness, as well as the cold it brings, overwhelms their ability to cope. A total exertion of energy is required to battle the foe that takes the place of light for more than two-thirds of the hours of an early winter's day.

But John draws a parallel between the light that dawned at creation and the light of redemption that dawns through the divine Word, Jesus Christ. The sin that permeates the world and corrupts the human heart is a darkness analogous to the chaos that reigned before God caused the first light to shine. Sin causes the same confusion, panic, and insanity in the spirit that coldness and deprivation of light cause in the body.

John's message is that the light of hope and salvation has come in Jesus. Jesus' birth brings truth to a world enslaved by deception. The Messiah comes to replace corruption with integrity, brokenness with wholeness, grief with joy.

The birth of the light of Christ is forever new. John emphasizes this by changing from the past to the present tense in verse five. The light of Christ is continually in action; it never ceases to shine.[2] Because Christ drives out the darkness of sin, death, and despair, he is the light of hope and life.

The modern world needs this message; it will never know the adventure of the spiritual romance without it. The domination of darkness in the modern world stymies not only the quest for individual well-being, but the search for collective justice and peace as well. Darkness is not present in scattered bits and pieces today; it covers everything like a blanket. It is an intrusive and imposing force that can only be managed, not mastered, by artificial means. An analogy reveals why: At midnight you can turn on a light in one room of your house, but unless you have lights on in all of the other rooms as well, that one light will not be strong enough to cast out all of the darkness.

And so it is in life. If not kept in check, evil dominates. Just as darkness obscures the vision of the eye, so evil blunts the vision of the soul. We do not see as we should. The problem is not with desire; it's with ability. The darkness of evil within us and around us cripples our sense of sight. Spiritually and morally handicapped, we do not understand ourselves, others, or God with the clarity or insight needed for authentic enlightenment.

An example of the dominating presence of darkness is found in the ways people treat one another. Insensitivity smothers the romance of the manger's hope. As the wise pastoral counselor Edward V. Stein has observed, the more complicated and busy our lives become, the more we lose touch with the humanness in one another. The person in the car in the next lane becomes an obstacle to our progress. The pedestrian in the crosswalk represents a hindrance that slows us down.

Too often we value other people according to what they can do for us or give to us, not according to who they are as God's children. Because we are so intent on climbing the ladder of success and achieving happiness according to our culture's materialistic values, we are always in a hurry. Time is money, and people have become a means to an end, not ends in themselves. The salesperson at the store is a voice-with-answers; the cashier at the counter, a hand-with-money; the child in the home, a nuisance-with-need.

But this is not how it was meant to be. Human beings were created to represent God's presence on earth, to show forth the light of God's love. When love abdicates, evil dominates. Evil's darkness robs people of their dignity. First it depersonalizes them; then it dehumanizes them. Finally, it becomes powerful enough to destroy them.

Sometimes the domination of evil is subtle, as in the small ways we fail to respect one another. At other times, evil becomes blatant. Poverty and war, racism and sexism, pornography and addiction, personal greed and domestic violence, environmental abuse and political corruption—these are but a few of the blatant injustices perpetrated by the forces of evil.

Christ came to show us a different way. He is the light who blesses life with the warmth of dignity. Now evil can no longer dominate the world with the chill of its treachery. No matter how frigid the night of injustice and indifference, it cannot hold back the dawning of a new day. The light of Christ provides the warmth in which the romance of hope can deepen and grow. Walls of alienation come down; trust is restored.

In the warmth of hope's romance, the influence of goodness expands. People and nations learn to respect one another. The tension in strained relationships eases. The future begins to look brighter than ever before. All of this becomes possible because in a manger in Bethlehem God spoke in Jesus Christ, the Word made flesh, and said, "Put that light back! Put back the light of goodness so that the human family can live in peace."

No More Intimidation

The light of Christ must be strong and resilient because the same darkness that tries to dominate the world also intimidates its people. Children are not the only ones afraid of the dark. In our own way, we are all afraid. That is why many of us have alarms in our homes; we don't want to be surprised in the darkness by an unwelcome intruder. It is also why we build prisons and try to protect ourselves and those we love from violent people and dangerous environments.

The darkness of evil intimidates us. I learned this for myself on a particularly hot summer night that I will never forget. There had been some break-ins in our neighborhood, and everyone seemed to be on edge. Since it was so hot, my wife and I were sleeping with our windows open, even though the bedroom windows are so low to the ground that a burglar could easily enter through one of them.

On this particular night, my wife went to bed early; I did not follow until around midnight. When I entered the bedroom, I was groping in the dark to find my way, all the while trying to be quiet. Suddenly my wife sat up in bed, threw off the covers, and began screaming at the top of her lungs. My first thought was that someone had broken in and was attacking her. I braced myself for a fight and searched frantically for the light switch. When I found the switch and turned it on, we could see we were alone. Carol had been having a bad dream. In the darkness, she did not know who I was; she thought I was some sinister intruder who was about to do her harm.

As the light illuminated the room, we stared at each other in a state of shock, gripped by a sense of panic that went beyond fear. Our stomachs churned, our adrenalin flowed, and our faces looked as white as the sheets on the bed. We were visibly shaken. The power of the darkness to play upon our worst fears had so intimidated us that we needed to stay up for some time before we regained our composure. Returning to bed was an act of courage; the mystery of the dark had penetrated our defenses and robbed us of our calm.

Many people share this feeling of intimidation, and for good reason. According to the Justice Department, one out of every three households in this country is affected by some kind of serious crime in a typical year. The nightly news never fails to report some heart-wrenching story of human tragedy and the evil that caused it. The home securities industry is one of the fastest growing in the country. Statistics show that the United States is the most violent country in the industrialized world. In 1990 a dozen cities—from Boston to New Orleans to Oakland—broke homicide records. For 15- to 19-year-old black males, the homicide rate has increased 99 percent since 1984. In some places metal detectors are used to confiscate weapons from high school students.[3]

The intimidation factor looms large today. In a world tainted by evil, we feel vulnerable and afraid. At first glance the Christmas story may not bring us much comfort; it is full of terror. A closer look, however, reveals that the light of Christ helps people manage their fears. God sends an angel to Zechariah, to Mary, and to the shepherds to tell them of their role in the Christmas drama, and they are all terrified. But in each instance, what does the angel say? He says, "Do not be afraid."

What a hollow admonition that would be without the assurance of God's presence with us. Only a fool is fearless in the face of real danger. To tell someone not to be afraid is futile unless the words are accompanied by evidence that there is nothing to fear. The Christmas event provides us with such evidence. Christ was born in order to break evil's power, and that is what he did. He resisted evil when he was tempted in the desert. He denounced evil when he confronted it in the Pharisees and in the corrupt political and economic systems of his day. He cast out evil when he encountered it in the insane and the possessed.

The light of Christ has broken the power of darkness. His work of liberation began in the manger but was completed at the cross and the empty tomb. As God's Word made flesh, Christ has come as concrete evidence that we need not be intimidated. As powerful as the darkness is in its most vicious forms—meaninglessness and isolation, depression and fatigue, disillusionment and anxiety, sickness and suffering, death and despair—it cannot extinguish the light of Christ.

John emphasizes the greater power of the light: "But to all who received him, who believed in his name," says John, "he gave *power* to become children of God, who were born, not of blood or of the will of the flesh or of the will of man, but of God" (John 1:12-13, italics added). These are important words because they focus on a Christian's identity. No one who is intimidated by the darkness can know the joy of hope's romance. To live in a state of intimidation is to live too tentatively and anxiously to be a person of hope.

The light of Christ reminds us of the ultimate victory that is ours. We have good reason not to be afraid because the mightiest power in all of creation has come to earth to take our side. Now we are children of the light, and no darkness can intimidate us forever.

A story in the *Wall Street Journal* some time ago dramatized this point in the personal experience of a flight attendant named Susan White. Susan White was one of the few survivors on United Airlines Flight 232, which crashed near Sioux City, Iowa, in the summer of 1989, killing 112 people. After the crash she suffered from posttraumatic stress. Her terrifying ordeal had burned into her memory a ghoulish scene of destruction and death.

Susan could not forget the horror of seeing parts of the plane scattered all over an Iowa corn field, of debris strewn everywhere, and of dead bodies, some still strapped to their seats, lying all around. Struggling with feelings of anger, guilt, and depression, she began having intimidating nightmares about random, violent death. She would dream she was in a plane that was crashing. Again she would see the faces and crumpled bodies of the dead and hear the shrieks of the children.

Susan could not work for a time, not because she was afraid of flying, but of landing. It took several months before she finally felt strong enough to return to her job. As these words from the *Wall Street Journal* attest, the presence of light helped Susan cope with the intimidating effects of her horrifying ordeal and nightmares:

> On her first DC-10 flight, she boarded early, paused at the seats located where passengers died last July, and cried once more. But on the return trip, she felt well enough to put on an apron and help the attendants staffing the flight.
>
> On a recent hop from Cleveland to Chicago, the morning darkness was lifting. Out the left window, the sun was rising above a velvety floor of purple clouds. Susan White looked out and smiled. "This is why I love flying," she said.[4]

The light of the manger's romance empowers people to stand against intimidation. Christ was born to drive away the nightmares of life's darkest moments. Back on the first Christmas, God looked down on our troubled world and said, "Put that light back!" Now we can walk in the light of Christ, the light that helps us move from timidity to tenacity. His light will not always protect us from harm or hurt, but it will always shine brightly enough in our hearts to assure us we are not alone. In the security of this assurance, hope is never far away.

No More Suffocation

It is the evil in the world that causes fear, but if the truth be told, much of this evil originates in the human heart and has a suffocating effect on goodness. All of us struggle with destructive habits that we cannot overcome.

We are plagued by hurtful attitudes and beset by volatile emotions.

What has happened to the celebration of Christmas is an outward example of this inward problem. At its best this season should be one of generosity in which people discover the joy of sharing. Instead, Christmas has become a time of exploitative commercialism and outright greed, a reflection of the imperfection of human nature.

The problem was highlighted in a cartoon that appeared on the editorial page of the *Providence Journal-Bulletin* in December of 1988. The cartoon pictures an extra-robust Santa Claus with a little boy seated on his lap. The boy's words are classic. He says to Santa, "Last year, if you recall, I asked for a bazooka, a computerized toy terrorist robot, an Uzi, a laser-guided nuclear obliterator and what did I get? A Rambo killer doll and a few paltry death darts! One more slip like that and you sleep with the fishes, fat boy!"[5]

Another example that contains an ironic truth is of the little boy who was being taught the Lord's Prayer. When he came to the part about "trespasses," he got it wrong and prayed, "Forgive us our *Christmases* as we forgive those who *Christmas* against us."

The presence of darkness in our hearts turns the best into the worst. Success becomes pride. Love becomes lust. Graciousness becomes greed. John suggests that the problem begins when we reject the light of Christ. There is tragedy in the words of John 1:11, "He came to what was his own, and his own people did not accept him."

We do not reject the Babe in the manger; he is helpless and harmless enough to win our hearts. We reject the adult Christ, the one who speaks of justice for the poor, who calls us to love the outcasts, and who holds us to such a high moral standard that we want to be rid of him.

We would rather trust the lesser light of our own intelligence and ingenuity than surrender completely to

Jesus Christ. The light of his goodness within us is often suffocated by our human nature. He invites us to wholeness in faith, but accepting his invitation means walking with him on the path of discipleship, and that involves putting others before ourselves; it involves sharing rather than hoarding, hungering for righteousness rather than riches, being a peacemaker behind the scenes rather than a celebrity whose name is always in the headlines.

It has become increasingly difficult to be a follower of Jesus Christ in America. What Christopher Lasch called "the culture of narcissism" in the late 1970s has become even more so today. Vanity reigns. On a large scale, people are preoccupied with the pursuit of personal peace and affluence. The worlds of sports, entertainment, business, and government have become more glitzy than ever before. People respond to glitz as a means of escape. They need somewhere to turn to leave behind the overwhelming stresses and crises of the times. So they look for relief to environments and personalities more exciting than their own. Amidst this escapist mentality the schools have never been weaker, families have never been more unstable, and relationships of all kinds have never been more transitory.

The ethic of self-preservation dominates popular thought. In the age of diminishing resources, people want to feel secure. The desire for security turns work into a religion, ulcers into status symbols, and success into an idol. Observing these misplaced priorities, the comedian George Carlin says that home is now the place where we keep our "stuff" while we go out and get "more stuff." In a more serious vein, the Lutheran pastor Gordon Dahl contends that in America we worship our work, work at our play, and play at our worship. The light of Christ is suffocated by such distorted priorities. As a result, people find themselves in the darkness, mentally and physically fatigued, and spiritually dead.

Some Americans seem determined to imitate the man in Loren Eiseley's book *The Invisible Pyramid*. During the New York City blackout of 1965, this man was trapped in the darkness on an upper floor of a skyscraper. Feeling his way, he managed to find a candle in his office desk. Since the elevators were not working, he began searching for a stairway. Finally he saw what appeared to be a small service doorway near the cluster of elevators. Holding his candle at eye level, he opened the door and stepped in. The next day, he was found at the bottom of an elevator shaft, the extinguished candle still clutched in his hand.[6]

Tragically, we find ourselves in this same condition when we follow the world's priorities rather than the light of Christ. Without him, the darkness within us becomes so thick that we can no longer breathe or see our way to walk on the liberating path of grace and truth.

In the Christmas miracle, God addressed our need. Jesus' birth in a rugged stable in Bethlehem was God's way of saying, "Put that light back! Put back the light of forgiveness so that the human soul is delivered from the suffocating effects of sin. Put back the light of spiritual awareness so that where there was once the brokenness of estrangement there can now be the wholeness of reconciliation."

This is the romance of the manger's hope. On the first Christmas, God looked down on the whole human family as it was being dominated and intimidated and suffocated by the darkness of evil, and God said, "I won't let it happen! I will send forth prophets to herald the coming of a day of light. I will give that day a place in history that no other can rival. I will announce the day's dawning on the voices of angels. I will share its glory with shepherds in the fields, and life on earth will never be the same."

That's what happened when Mary gave birth to

her firstborn son and wrapped him in swaddling cloths and laid him in a manger. Today he is the Christ, the light that shines forever in the window, and the darkness has not—and cannot—overcome it.

Prayer for the Sunday After Christmas

O God of mangers and mysteries, we receive this Sunday
after Christmas as a gift from your hand.
Rather than lament the ending of a season of celebration,
we welcome the beginning of Christ's
continuing reign in our lives.
The grace and truth that you revealed in his coming have
surprised us with joy.
In Jesus, you have awakened us to the promise of divine
love and the possibility of earthly peace.
He has brought light into the world and into our lives.
In the comforting warmth and undimmed lustre of his
light, we sense your presence.

We seek you, faithful God, as people who have just
completed one journey and now begin another.
Lead us on, we pray.
Just as we followed you to Bethlehem, where our hearts
were filled with the wonder of the Christmas miracle,
so would we now trust your light to guide us back
home,
back to the everyday disciplines of life and faith,
where joy is often hard to find amid overdue
bills and frantic schedules, amid demanding
relationships and unfinished projects.

You know, dear God, that we are like the shepherds, with
lives full of responsibilities.
We are busy and preoccupied, like the innkeeper, and
continually searching for new meaning, like the
Magi.
Yet we venture forth into the new year in the confidence
that your peace rests upon us.

The Christmas bells are still ringing,
   the star in the heavens still shining.
      Angels never stop announcing the good news,
         and the Christ child continues to dwell among us
            through the witness of your Spirit.

Thank you, God of glory, that you go with us into all of
   the seasons of our lives.
   In our rising up and lying down,
      our going out and coming in,
      our moments of celebration as well as desperation,
   you have promised never to leave or forsake us.

May we be attentive to your light not only when
   circumstances are favorable,
      but also when the darkness descends, with all of its
         dominating, intimidating, and suffocating
         power,
   to assault our vulnerable hearts.

Persevere with us on our journey of faith, that fear and
         uncertainty may give way to confidence and
         hope.

Enter our thinking and our dreaming, our believing and
         our living, that we might find the discipline and
         commitment to follow our Emmanuel, even
         Jesus Christ our Lord, in whose name we pray.
         AMEN.

Questions for Reflection and Study

1. To set the first chapter of John in its larger biblical context, explore such passages as Psalms 27:1; 36:9; Isaiah 9:2-7; John 8:12; 12:35; 2 Corinthians 4:6; and Revelation 21:23. Discuss the various ways in which the metaphor of light is applied in the course of God's self-revelation. Take a moment to enumerate the specific themes associated with light and try to describe each of them with one word. Given the fact that these themes are all overwhelmingly hopeful and triumphant in nature, what implications does this have for what attitudes Christians should adopt and what spirit they should display to others?

2. There are some biblical texts in which the metaphor of light is given a distinctively ethical interpretation. That is to say, light is employed as an ideal that describes who we should be and how we should live. Among these texts are Psalm 112:4-10; Isaiah 8:6-9; Matthew 5:14-16; Romans 13:11-14; and Ephesians 5:6-20. What is the relationship between the themes contained in these texts and John's description of Jesus as the light? In what way does Jesus Christ inform the Christian ethical life?

3. It was suggested in this chapter that the light of Christ can help believers cope with the dominating, intimidating, and suffocating effects of both physical and spiritual darkness. After pausing for a time of personal reflection, share with the rest of the group whether or not the themes of domination, intimidation, and suffocation are relevant to your experience of darkness. If you do not find these themes relevant, share why. If

you do, share your experience of specific instances in which the illuminating power of Christ's light sustained you amidst an encounter with darkness.

4. The prologue to John's Gospel is one of the most philosophical parts of the New Testament. It deals with the mystery of the Logos, the revealed Word of God who is Jesus Christ. Explore the meaning of the idea of the Word of God in the Old Testament by reading the following passages: Genesis 1:1-3; Psalms 33:6-9; 107:20; 147:15-18; Ezekiel 37:1-5; Isaiah 55:10-11; Jeremiah 1:4, 11; and 2:1. In these texts, what are some of the functions of the Word of God? What are some of the Word's attributes? How can these functions and attributes be related to Jesus Christ? What are some practical implications of the concept of the Word of God for the Christian life?

5. Theologian Jürgen Moltmann offers the following explanation of the purpose of the incarnation:

> *Self-communicating love* . . . only becomes fulfilled, blissful love when its love is returned. That is why the Father finds bliss in the eternal response to his love through the Son. If he communicates his love for the Son creatively through him to the one who is other than himself, then he also desires to find bliss through this other's responsive love.[7]

Have you ever associated the idea of bliss with God? If not, how might a deepened understanding of the ecstasy of love shared among the members of the Trinity affect your view of God and of faith? How would you live your life differently if you developed a new awareness of the joy your love for God brings to God? What implications might a vital experience of bliss have for a Christian's practice of the disciplines of worship, study, and service?

6. The publication of the book *The Myth of God Incarnate* (John Hick, ed., [Philadelphia: Westminster Press, 1977]) sparked a new debate about Christology (the systematic study of the person and work of Jesus Christ). The authors of this book argued that the incarnation has importance as a religious myth but cannot be defended as a historical reality. By contrast, Dietrich Bonhoeffer insisted that it is counterproductive to concentrate on the "Alchemy of the Incarnation." It is only helpful to explore questions about what, where, and who is Jesus Christ. This exploration, in turn, only makes sense as one personally experiences God's saving power in Jesus as it is known in Word, sacrament, church, and community. In other words, the only understanding of the divinity of the Son of God that really matters is the understanding that becomes real through personal encounter.

Can the view advanced in *The Myth of God Incarnate* be reconciled with Bonhoeffer's view? How might a decision to take one side or the other affect the formation of one's faith? What are the dangers involved in rejecting belief in Jesus' divinity? And what are the dangers of overemphasizing his divinity at the expense of his humanity?

---

[1] See David H.C. Read, *I Am Persuaded* (New York: Charles Scribner's Sons, 1961), pp. 149-150.

[2] Leon Morris, *The Gospel According to John* (Grand Rapids: William B. Eerdmans Publishing Co., 1971), p. 85.

[3] "Violence in the Cities," *Christian Science Monitor,* December 13, 1990, p. 20.

[4] Laurie McGinley, "Fear of Landing," *Wall Street Journal,* January 18, 1990, p. A6.

[5] *Providence Journal-Bulletin,* December 10, 1988, p. A-14. © *Miami News,* 1987.

[6] Loren Eiseley, *The Invisible Pyramid* (London: Rupert Hart-Davis Ltd., 1971), pp. 82-83.

[7] Jürgen Moltmann, *The Trinity and the Kingdom* (San Francisco: Harper and Row, 1981), p. 117.

seven

Epiphany's Invitation to Intimacy

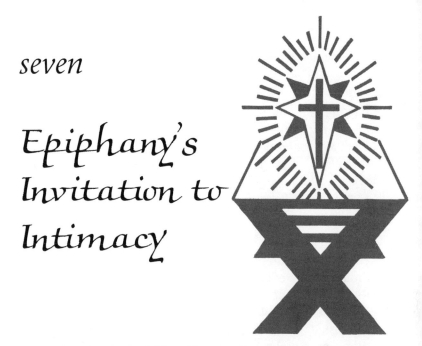

In the time of King Herod, after Jesus was born in Bethlehem of Judea, wise men from the East came to Jerusalem, asking, "Where is the child who has been born king of the Jews? For we observed his star at its rising, and have come to pay him homage." When King Herod heard this, he was frightened, and all Jerusalem with him; and calling together all the chief priests and scribes of the people, he inquired of them where the Messiah was to be born. They told him, "In Bethlehem of Judea; for so it has been written by the prophet:

'And you, Bethlehem, in the land of Judah,
   are by no means least among the rulers of
      Judah;
   for from you shall come a ruler
      who is to shepherd my people Israel.' "

Then Herod secretly called for the wise men and learned from them the exact time when the star had appeared. Then he sent them to Bethlehem, saying, "Go and search diligently for the child; and when you have found him, bring me word so that I may also go and pay him homage." When they had heard the king, they set out; and there, ahead of them, went the star that they had seen at its rising, until it stopped over the place where the child was. When they saw that the star

107

had stopped, they were overwhelmed with joy. On entering the house, they saw the child with Mary his Mother; and they knelt down and paid him homage. Then, opening their treasure chests, they offered him gifts of gold, frankincense, and myrrh. And having been warned in a dream not to return to Herod, they left for their own country by another road.

—Matthew 2:1-12

In the fall of 1990 Americans witnessed an extraordinary media event. The Public Broadcasting Service aired for the first time its highly acclaimed documentary on the Civil War. Since I live in Rhode Island, I was particularly interested in the important contributions that two Civil War–era Rhode Islanders made to the series. One of them, Elisha Hunt Rhodes, was a former deacon and superintendent of the Sunday school at Central Baptist Church, Providence, where I serve as pastor. His diaries were quoted extensively.

The other Rhode Islander who received much attention was Sullivan Ballou, an obscure major in the Union Army. A week before the Battle of Bull Run in 1861, Major Ballou wrote home to his wife Sarah in Smithfield. His letter, which was read during the PBS series, stirred the hearts of all who heard it. Major Ballou's love for his wife, and his confidence that they would meet again in either this life or the next, testify to the power of both romance and hope. His tender words at a time of impending crisis are unforgettable:

> But, O Sarah! If the dead can come back to this earth and the unseen around those they loved, I shall always be near you; in the gladdest days and in the darkest nights . . . always, always, and if there be a soft breeze upon your cheek, it shall be my breath, as the cool air fans your throbbing temple, it shall be my spirit passing by. Sarah, do not mourn me dead; think I am gone and wait for thee, for we shall meet again.[1]

A Universal Yearning

I have a suspicion about why Sullivan Ballou's words struck such an emotional chord in those who heard them. Not only do they bear witness to love's triumph over war and death, they also describe the kind of intimacy that everyone longs for but few find. In a different, more powerful sense Epiphany is also about intimacy. It's about the intimacy that the gospel establishes between Christ and his people.

Epiphany declares that the gospel is for everyone. The light of Christ has been manifested for all to see. The romance of hope has reached its culmination.

When the Magi followed the star to Bethlehem, they represented all of humanity. They were engaged in the universal human search for intimacy with God. Epiphany is a time of joy because it celebrates the reward of their efforts. Theirs was a spiritual journey that began in hope and ended in fulfillment. At home, they knew the inner restlessness that accompanies the quest for spiritual illumination; at the manger, they found peace.

Everyone is now invited to go with the Magi on a journey that holds untold challenge and promise for all who take it. Those who persevere until the end will find wholeness in God through Jesus Christ.

Human romance is but a crude imitation of the deeper yearning for this spiritual communion. We begin a romantic relationship hoping it will lead to a complete sharing of life with another. We long to love and be loved in such a way that we feel fulfilled and secure. The promise that this journey will lead to intimacy motivates us to keep traveling, with romance and hope our companions.

But something always gets in the way. The healing, transforming, and empowering bond that two vulnerable spirits seek is elusive; it is found only rarely. Such a bond cannot be contrived; it is formed spontaneously, mysteriously.

The fortunate few find the bond in marriage, but

most do not. Many never experience it in any relationship because their human frailties prevent its growth. Still, nearly everyone continues to believe in and desire this fulfilling relational bliss.

The quest for oneness with another nurtures the romantic impulse in the same way that a yearning for God enlivens faith. One reason the story of the Magi has endured so long is that it has romance at its heart, a much more powerful romance than the one that led Sullivan Ballou to write his impassioned letter to his wife. What could be more romantic than the quest to follow a star to encounter the living Christ?

Life in the Far Country

However, like all great love stories, Epiphany is as much about separation as about communion. It begins with the experience of estrangement. The Magi were not of the chosen race; they were foreigners. They lived in a far country (many scholars think it was Persia) and did not follow the Law or revere the covenants.

It is traditionally thought that the Magi were three in number because they brought three gifts—gold, frank-incense, and myrrh. But no one actually knows how many Magi there were. What is certain, however, is that they were not kings (as claimed by the popular Christmas carol), but astrologers.

The Magi were among the most educated people of their day, learned in the areas of philosophy, literature, and science. They continually studied the constellations of the heavens because they believed the movements of the stars and planets would give them insight into the nature of God and the meaning of life.

Anyone who has ever felt excluded or known the pain of alienation in romance should be able to identify with the Magi—and that is all of us. For much of their lives, time and place separated them from an intimate experience of God's love. They sought this love from a distance, far removed from its vital center.

How frustrating it must have been always to be on the outside looking in. As Gentiles, the Magi knew the pain of separation, which, as Erich Fromm says in *The Art of Loving*, results in emotional chaos within. "Being separate," writes Fromm, "means being cut off, without any capacity to use my human powers. Hence to be separate means to be helpless, unable to grasp the world—things and people—actively; it means that the world can invade me without my ability to react. Thus, separateness is the source of intense anxiety. Beyond that, it arouses shame and the feeling of guilt."[2]

There is no greater loneliness than to be separated from love. One feels isolated, empty, forlorn. Self-esteem plummets and quiet desperation sets in. The desperation follows on the heels of long silences that no voice interrupts. It intrudes at social gatherings when a person without a partner feels out of place. It greets people who dread going home at night to an empty house, who experience eating dinner and going to bed alone as a painful ordeal.

The desperation of being separated from love stems from the feeling that no one cares, that when you die you will not be missed, that it will be as if you had never lived. Amidst such feelings, life becomes a trial to be endured rather than a gift to be cherished and shared.

Such was the experience of separation that the Magi knew. A boy named Bobby in Michael Cunningham's novel *A Home at the End of the World* describes the experience well. Bobby wants and needs closeness with his suicidal mother, but never finds it. He remembers how "once, when she passed me in the hall on her way to the bathroom, she stopped long enough to stroke my hair. She didn't speak. She looked at me as if she was standing on a platform in a flat, dry country and I was pulling away on a train that traveled high into an alpine world."[3]

Do you feel the pain of that image? You want and need closeness with another person, but instead it is as if you are on a train and the person you love is "standing on a platform in a flat, dry country" as the train pulls out of the station. This feeling haunts many relationships between family members and friends and lovers. It is particularly painful in romance because it involves grief over what could have been. Thoughts of intimate moments that will not be shared pierce the heart, or memories that cannot be relived plague the mind.

Throughout our lives we try to protect ourselves from getting hurt, but sometimes the hurt comes anyway. It is one thing to find romance; it is another to sustain it in a secure, growing relationship. More often than not, romance falls victim to personality conflicts or shattered expectations, to unfulfilled needs or outside pressures, to changing interests or competing attractions. In order to survive, it must transcend these potential snares. It must also rise above petty jealousies and find ways to exorcise the demon of boredom.

If these pitfalls threaten human romance, how much more they also endanger our relationship with God. The divine lover of our souls continually woos us, but we are slow to respond. The waywardness of our hearts alienates us from our first love; we feel the pain of separation.

Like the Magi, at a deeper level than we can even comprehend, we long for intimacy with God. There is a hunger in our souls that only God can satisfy, a thirst that only God can quench. But whether by open rebellion or a failure to surrender completely to the divine romance, we remain distant from the Source of life. Our tendency to stray from our spiritual roots keeps us wandering in what Jesus (in the story of the prodigal son) called "the far country," estranged from the healing and renewing power of wholeness in him.

The Magi found themselves in a similar situation. From a distance, they had seen glimmers of divine love's radiance. They knew there was a creative force behind the glories of nature and the sensitivities of their own spirits. From their vantage point in the far country, they kept watching for some sign that God was alive and loved them.

After years of waiting, the sign finally came. On an ordinary night, a night that probably began just like every other night, they looked up into the heavens and saw a star. It was not just any star; it was *the* star, the one that appeared to announce the birth of God's Messiah.

A Symbol's Call to Reverence

Stars are often present in stories of romance; they sparkle above as lovers kiss and dream and share tender moments. It seems fitting that a star would figure prominently in the Epiphany drama, which celebrates the romance of the manger.

The Magi needed a star to follow. As they journeyed to Bethlehem, they moved from the darkness of separation from God to the light of worship in Christ's presence. Their secular ideals could not lead them to this worship; only God could. By following the star, they found him whose moral values and sacrificial love would make intimacy with God possible for all.

But such intimacy can only be realized after a long journey, a journey taken in stages. One stage involves reverence for life, a profound respect for the dignity and worth of every person. When the Magi made their way to Bethlehem, they did so in a brutal and uncaring world. The Roman armies were on the march. Slavery was a harsh reality for thousands. Women had no rights; they were the property of their husbands. Taxes were high and wages low. The finer things of life were reserved for the privileged few while the underprivileged masses struggled merely to survive. It was a world of poverty and disease and suffering. But it was a world that would be illumined by the presence of Jesus, just as the shining star illumined the Judean night.

The Magi traveled to Bethlehem in search of the Christ, the one who would inaugurate a new order. The star announced that the old order was passing away, that the forces of brutality and oppression and brokenness would one day be defeated by God's triumphant love.

The Magi found encouragement in the unspoken yet vital message that pulsated from the star's silent radiance. It was the message that the world should be a better place—and could be a better place—if people would only treat one another with the respect and understanding they deserve as God's children.

This theme was central to the message Christ came to preach. The star's position high in the heavens can be seen as a metaphor of how his emphasis on human dignity and worth would lift humanity's moral vision to new heights. His coming brought the promise of a day in which there would be no more war, no more violence, no more injustice of any kind.

The star made the promise of this day visible for everyone to see. It shone on through the night to call all people into the kind of intimacy with God that nurtures reverence for life. When such reverence reigns in every heart, Christ's promise of peace will be fulfilled.

Until then, we have been given a star to follow. The Epiphany story is a parable of the human quest for peace in communion with God. I am glad that the story involves a star, because stars are bright and mysterious and fascinating. Surely the Magi must have found this one so; otherwise they could not have followed it so long and so far.

Stars are gifts from God that people sing about and wish upon. It is only natural that a star would shine forth in Epiphany's story of joy and promise. Yet no one knows what the Magi actually saw shining in the East. Maybe a supernova, some say; possibly a conjunction of planets, say others. Or, suggest still others, the star could have been some natural or supernatural phenomena functioning within the earth's atmosphere.

All speculation aside, what the star *did* is more important than what it was. The star led the Magi out of the far country and showed them the way to Jesus Christ. It can play a similar role in our faith as it guides us toward the moral understanding and spiritual intimacy found at the manger.

We may be different from the Magi in many ways, but we have one desire in common with them: They were seeking wholeness in God and so are we. In this search, there are times when we need desperately to see a star and follow it. We set goals and live by values that we hope will lead us to fulfillment and peace. We want our relationships to bring us satisfaction in the good times and support in the bad.

But we easily go astray. Sometimes we settle for second-rate ideals and twisted relationships. Under the influence of a materialistic and self-centered culture, we do not reach higher because we mistakenly think it is to our advantage not to. Ted Koppel pointed out the fallacy of this attitude in his commencement address at Duke University, in which he said:

> We have actually convinced ourselves that slo-
> gans will save us. Shoot up if you must, but use
> a clean needle. Enjoy sex whenever and with
> whomever you wish, but wear a condom. No!
> The answer is no. Not because it isn't cool or
> smart or because you might end up in jail or
> dying in an AIDS ward, but no because it's
> wrong, because we have spent 5,000 years as a
> race of rational human beings, trying to drag our-
> selves out of the primeval slime by searching for
> truth and moral absolutes. In its purest form,
> truth is not a polite tap on the shoulder. It is a
> howling reproach. What Moses brought down
> from Mount Sinai were not the Ten Suggestions.[4]

Jesus was born not to abolish the moral Law of God, but to fulfill it. The sacredness of life and of human beings is one of the Law's abiding ideals. The Epiphany star appeared in the heavens to remind us of this sacredness and to lead us to embrace Jesus' ethic of love.

Unfortunately, as someone has said, "It is hard to see the star of Bethlehem in a universe of man-made satellites." We need Epiphany every year to restore and sharpen our vision. When that vision is lifted high enough to see the promise of God's kingdom in the Messiah's birth, it will fill our lives with hope.

The Magi brought their gifts to Jesus in response to the hope they saw in the star. Their gifts honored not only who he was, but also what he came to stand for. In reverencing him, they reverenced the best and the highest in life itself.

Engaging the Fight

In order for the Magi to reach their destination, their faith also had to mature to the stage of strategic defiance. They practiced the discipline of believing against all odds. Because they were not part of the Jewish community, they received little support in their search for the Messiah. They engaged in a highly unpopular religious quest without reliable teachings and traditions to guide them.

But the Magi would not be deterred. As the high-minded idealists of their day, they stood firm against the status quo. Many of their contemporaries did not even believe in one transcendent and almighty God, let alone a God who loved the world enough to send it a Savior. The Magi, in contrast, heeded the voice of their consciences and depended on their internal resilience to sustain their faith.

Their desire for an intimate encounter with God in the infant Jesus inspired them to persevere. They knew that in order for life to be full and meaningful it must have a quest for truth at its center. In this knowledge, they committed themselves to the Bethlehem journey, and even Herod's treachery could not make them quit and go home.

Romance often meets opposition, just as the Magi met Herod. A love story would be boring without the element of danger in it. What brings the plot to life is the presence of some force that threatens to keep the lovers apart. Perhaps the force is a gang rivalry, as in *West Side Story*. Or maybe it is parental disapproval, as in *Fiddler on the Roof*, or a raging civil war, as in *Gone with the Wind*. The threatening force plays as active a role in the story as the lovers themselves.

In real life, our own emotions pose an ominous threat to romance. Anger and jealousy, selfishness and pride, melancholy and negativity—these forces, when uncontrolled, can destroy even the strongest relationship. As the author Robert Anderson says of love in marriage, "In every marriage more than a week old, there are grounds for divorce. The trick is to find, and continue to find, grounds for marriage."[5]

At some point, if romance is to succeed, the people involved must commit themselves to defying these hostile forces. A strategy must be devised to engage the fight. If a couple fails to unite in battle against their common foes, they will inevitably turn on each other and romance will die, a victim of self-inflicted wounds.

Mary and Jim, for instance, will only survive as a couple if they fight as one against Jim's growing dependence on alcohol. The enemy that threatens Gail and Charles's romance is their overly demanding work schedules. Lucy and Stephen have been buffeted by an affair that Lucy has had. Clara and Ed have not listened to each other for years, criticizing each other instead. Each of these couples must band together against the forces that would destroy their relationship. The survival of love requires a solid alliance; it survives by becoming defiant.

Achieving the Goal

Out of defiance arises hope, the kind of hope that kept the Magi searching until they found the Christ. Herod represented a hostile threat to their quest to encounter incarnate love, but they refused to be intimidated. They defied all odds and pressed on to their goal. Conquering the foes of distance and darkness and danger, they arrived to present their gifts to the holy Child. In return, they received the greater gift of having been in his presence.

The experience of the Magi shows that the journey toward Christ always involves struggle and risk. Many forces, from the seductions of the world to our own undisciplined use of time and mismanaged priorities, seek to keep us in the far country, alienated and alone. The journey can only continue as we honestly assess what we are up against and find the strength to defy the enemies of our spirits.

Matthew's telling of the Epiphany story suggests that the Magi had done this assessment and relied upon the strength that comes from God. They persevered against every threat to their faith and welfare. With fierce determination and defiant hope, they followed the star to Bethlehem. Finding the child fulfilled their dream of intimate communion with the Source of all love, the Author of all joy. In the warmth and security of this spiritual communion, they were included as members of God's family. Through faith, they transcended their separateness and became whole in the liberating grace of Christ.

A comment on television by the novelist John Updike suggests a parallel to the Magi's experience. As he was being interviewed on camera, Updike was asked how he could reconcile the strong religious themes in his new book with its very realistic and candid treatment of sex. Updike responded that he didn't see any contradiction between the two at all. In fact, he went on to say, "People go to church because they want to live forever. They go to bed because they want to feel what it's like."[6]

Updike has a point. Although sex is trivialized today in every medium from television and the movies to popular novels and tabloid newspapers, it is meant to be one of God's most sacred gifts. Two people expressing love as intimate partners in the context of commitment speaks of the greater love to be found in union with God. Just as romance culminates in sexual union, so does faith find its fulfillment in oneness with the divine.

Epiphany reminds us that the spiritual journey has this oneness as its ultimate goal. It is necessary to refer to the most pleasant, joyful, and intimate of all human experiences to describe the ecstasy that awaits the soul at rest in God.

Epiphany declares that Christ came to make the ecstasy of union with the divine available to all. The Epiphany star still illumines the spiritual journey; it invites everyone, everywhere, to follow the Prince of Peace. Those who follow him will encounter the romance of the manger. They will walk in hope, the kingdom of God ever before them.

Being a pilgrim on the way to the kingdom is life's greatest challenge and joy. The Magi came from afar. So must we. When our first step, as our last, is taken in faith, we will finally reach the goal and know abundant joy. The joy will be found in communion with Christ, the one who came as a vulnerable infant long ago, but who now reigns in heaven as Lord of all. Bring your gifts, as the Magi brought theirs. O come, let us adore him!

Prayer for Epiphany

With all of our praise and all of our pain,
    all of our joys and all of our fears,
    all of our hopes and all of our concerns,
        we come to you, O God of light.
We come in the spirit of the Magi, the spirit of curiosity
        and perseverance, of determination and faith.
Reveal yourself to us, we pray.

Whether we are living in harmony with your will and are
        deeply invested in the work of your kingdom,
or whether we are wandering in some far country of
        subtle alienation or open rebellion,
    we need you.
Every time we try to walk alone we stumble and fall.
In your presence we are brought to our senses. We realize
        how dependent we are on your goodness and
        grace.

We give thanks for the Epiphany message, which tells of
        your desire to include all people in your
        kingdom.
We worship you for who you are,
    the almighty Creator of the heavens and earth,
    yet the God who knows us so intimately that the very
        hairs on our heads are numbered.

We approach you like the Magi, watching from a distance
        for some sign of your coming that will fill our
        hearts with hope.
We rejoice that you have given us this sign in Jesus our
        Lord.
In the grace revealed in him, you look beyond our sins
        and love us unconditionally.
You accept us more readily and more fully than we accept
        ourselves.

You bring us from isolation to fellowship, from shame to
dignity, from death to life.

Challenge us each day, holy God, to reach high in our
quest to find Christ and to live by his teachings.
But catch us when we fall, we pray.
Keep the star of Bethlehem shining always in our hearts,
and lead us out of darkness into your marvelous
light.

Grant us the strength we need to follow, and give us eyes
discerning enough to see the goal ahead.
Send us faithful companions to walk the way with us.
But most of all, speak to us by your Spirit.

Speak from above and grant us a glimpse of your glory.
Speak from beyond and call us to the discipline of
committed faith.
Speak from within and remind us of the worthiness of the
journey.
Walk with us, and mold us, until we conform to the
image of your Son, the image of love that leads
to peace in communion with you. AMEN.

Questions for Reflection and Study

1. This chapter drew a parallel between the human romance that culminates in sexual intimacy and the spiritual romance that culminates in union with God. Explore this parallel futher by referring to Hosea 2:19-20; 2 Corinthians 11:2; Ephesians 5:26-27; and Revelation 21:2,9.

   What effect might a deeper awareness of the Bible's "marriage imagery" as related to Christ's relationship to the church and to believers have on your spiritual development? What are some of the implications of allowing your life to be intentionally molded by this imagery?

2. It has been suggested in this chapter that "reverence for life" and "strategic defiance" are two important themes in the story of the Magi. In what ways are these themes applicable to the Christian life in our time?

3. The journey of the Magi to Bethlehem is one of many journeys in the Bible. Compare Matthew 2:1-12 with the following texts: Genesis 12:1-9; Exodus 16:33-36; Ruth 1:1-22; Luke 2:1-7; and Acts 9:1-9. What are some of the common themes in these journey stories? What are the differences? How might the experiences described in these texts be relevant to your life?

4. How do the people involved in the journeys of the Bible cope with such things as circumstances beyond their control, uncertainty, and fatigue? In what ways is God's presence on the journey revealed? What are some of the lessons learned along the way? Why are

personal growth and the development of faith so often related to struggle and crisis in these stories?

5. On their journey to Bethlehem the Magi encountered the treachery of Herod. How did they respond, and why? Can you think of any biblical advice to believers, or do you recall other Bible stories of good people outsmarting bad, that would also be wise to heed?

6. What statement does Herod's presence in the Epiphany story make about the problem of evil in the spiritual life? Is there a sufficient balance between realism and idealism in this story, or is one or the other more prominent? What are the implications of your answer for how the Christan life should be lived and to what extent equality for all people can be achieved?

7. The world of the New Testament era was riddled with divisions along the lines of religion, race, class, and gender. One of the dominant themes of Epiphany is that God loves everyone equally and that these divisions reflect humanity's unenlightened condition. The story of the Magi is part of a larger biblical framework that stresses the inclusiveness of the gospel. Trace the development of this framework by studying the following themes and texts:
    Jesus' reference to his sheep of another fold:
        John 10:16
    Jesus' use of Samaritans as moral examples:
        Luke 10:25-37
        Luke 17:11-19
    Jesus' equal treatment of women:
        John 4:7-26
        Luke 8:1-3
        Luke 10:38-42

Paul's statement of radical equality for all:
Galatians 3:28
Paul's gospel for the Gentiles:
Ephesians 2:11-22

On what is the inclusiveness of the gospel based? In what ways does the church's failure to be inclusive hamper its ministry? What might result if the theme of inclusiveness were given more attention during the Epiphany season?

---

[1] "A Letter Home," *Boston Globe*, Sept. 29, 1990, p. 1. See also Geoffrey C. Ward with Ric Burns and Ken Burns, *The Civil War* (New York: Alfred A. Knopf, Inc., 1990), p. 83.

[2] Erich Fromm, *The Art of Loving* (New York: Bantam Books, 1956), p. 7.

[3] Michael Cunningham, *A Home at the End of the World* (New York: Farrar, Straus, and Giroux, 1990), p. 76.

[4] Ted Koppel, quoted in "Education: Now, a Few Words from the Wise," *Time*, June 22, 1987, p. 69.

[5] Robert Anderson, *Solitaire/Double Solitaire* (New York: Random House, 1972), p. 32.

[6] Quoted in David H. C. Read, "We Belong to God," *Best Sermons 1*, ed. James W. Cox (San Francisco: Harper and Row, 1988), p. 10.